AF255100

The Pimp and the Pork Sausage

SUSAN NORMAN

The Pimp and the Pork Sausage

A Story of Life

The Pimp and the Pork Sausage: A Story of Life
Susan Norman

© Copyright Susan Norman 2023

This book reflects the author's present recollections of experiences
over time. For various reasons some names, characteristics
and identifying details have been changed, some events have
been compressed, and some dialogue has been recreated.

All rights reserved. This book may not be reproduced in whole or
part, stored, posted on the internet, or transmitted in any form or
by any means, electronic, mechanical, photocopying, recording,
or other, without permission from the author of this book.

Typeset and cover design by BookPOD

ISBN: 978-0-6458398-0-7   eISBN: 978-0-6458398-1-4

A catalogue record for this
book is available from the
National Library of Australia

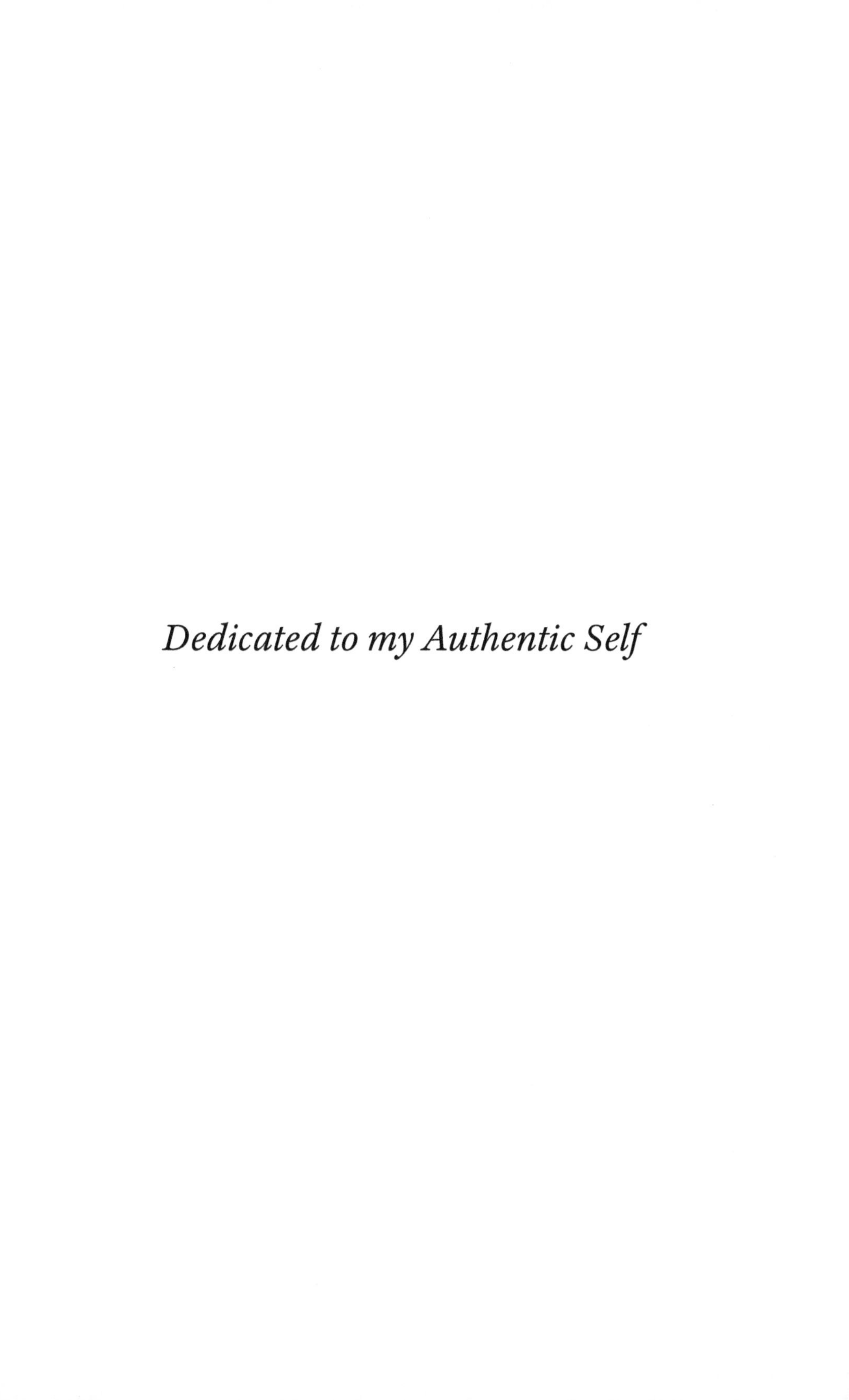

Dedicated to my Authentic Self

Acknowledgements

I owe an enormous debt of gratitude to Ruby. She has been, and still is, my rock. Cooking for me when she got home from school and I was still working at the panel beater's, sacrificing her Austudy payments so we could save for a new home, always being there when I needed her, and laughing kindly at my misspelt text messages. I regret the trauma she went through as a child when I may have been able to do better. I love her to pieces.

John, you are amazing. Your advice is solid and your support unwavering – thank you.

Martin and Diane Campion, your friendship was always there when I needed it – thank you.

Michael Collins, my ghostwriter and my friend – thank you. MCmemoirs.com.au

Rabbit – you're always there when I need you – thank you.

Author's comment

I have written this book in good faith. If I have misrepresented anyone, or been inaccurate with dates and places, I apologise. In certain circumstances, names have been changed.

Contents

Chapter 1   Early life
Children should be seen, then have the crap belted out of them   5

Chapter 2   Bob the Sailor
The Claytons dad   11

Chapter 3   School
First steps in a brilliant academic life   17

Chapter 4   Max
A marriage made in hell   23

Chapter 5   Poverty and violence
And pork sausages for the soul.   37

Chapter 6   Jeffery and Ruby
Innocence betrayed   55

Chapter 7   Australia
First steps to freedom   67

Chapter 8   Jeffery
A life of torment   79

Chapter 9   Prison
A career behind bars   95

Chapter 10   Robert
Real love   117

Chapter 11   Ivy
Developing an immunity   139

Chapter 12   The company
A hard won defeat.   143

Chapter 13   Friendship and family
The good and the bad   155

Chapter 14   Grandchildren
A second chance to do things better   171

Chapter 15   Susan
That's me, my authentic self   181

Prologue

I knew something was wrong before I witnessed the murder of Debra Dick, before she was stabbed to death with a sharpened barbeque fork. I was thirty-five years old and working in Boggo Road prison as an officer. The sun was burning down and two prisoners sat on the veranda, absentmindedly chatting, their words slipping between the concrete slats. It was lunchtime and they had just finished eating. Debra's friend's eyes fixated on some point in the distance as they sat. I didn't have much interaction with these two, but I knew that they were friends and that they liked drugs. And I knew that this is why Debra was killed.

The canteen was bustling with prisoners, the smell of hot food hanging in the fetid air. I stood by a wall, keeping watch over the room, my starched uniform pressing into my skin. I had a feeling something was going on. The inmates kept turning and looking, their eyes flickering from me to the other officers as they whispered between themselves. A knot twisted in my stomach. This wasn't normal.

I was facing in the other direction when I heard the first scream. Whipping around, I saw Storm Brooke and Amarlie Badenoch hunched over Debra and her friend, their arms violently thrashing back and forth above their crumpled bodies. Metal glinted in the sun, the weapons stabbing bolts of light across the room as they plunged into the soft skin of the women's backs. Blood erupted from the gashes. I sprinted across the room, adrenaline pulsing through my veins. Suddenly the alarm was blaring, a deafening cacophony of noise screeching through the quickly hardening atmosphere of the room. The other prisoners did nothing. They just carried on sitting at their tables watching the butchery unfold. They knew they couldn't get involved, or they might be next.

I flew towards the veranda, skirting around Debra as she bled out onto the floor, chair tipped backwards, her body warm, still living. There were other officers tending to her, trying to keep her alive, to stem the bleeding. But I knew I needed to stop the assailants. I barged across the floor, jolting to a stop outside the rec room and kitchen. I was suddenly face-to-face with the attackers. All the prisoners had collected there, standing and staring at me. Storm and Amarlie had wedged their way back into the herd among the other inmates, their faces blank, eyes silently boring into mine. I scanned the adjacent kitchen, looking for the lethal weapons. Poking out from under a metal drawer I saw the russet, bloodied points of the long, two-pronged carving utensils. In an instant I knew I couldn't touch them, knew that they'd be needed for evidence. My main concern now was ensuring no one else got hurt.

I wedged myself in front of the drawer, shielding the weapons with my body. Amarlie began pacing aggressively, growling, obviously agitated. Terror clawed at my pounding heart. I was putting myself between two murderers and the proof that would condemn them. I was alone. This was not a safe situation. I knew I couldn't move, though. If I did, she would grab the forks and find a way to dispose of the evidence. So I stayed put, rigid, waiting for an attack. Blood rushed through my ears and every movement felt electric, my vision sharp and focused. I was aware of every twitch, every sound, every glance thrown from prisoner to prisoner. No one was moving. It was a sea of statues except for Amarlie's restless pacing back and forth. The alarm was still blazing and I heard the clatter of footsteps. Three male officers arrived, one bursting into the room, immediately barging straight to the bins, rifling through them for the weapons. 'Stop!' I commanded, 'Don't touch anything!' He looked up, saw what I was guarding and moved back to join the other officers who were circling the room, their presence enforcing the finely balanced order I was trying to uphold.

I stayed there until the police came. My heart was still thudding, my body physically processing what I had just witnessed but my mind was solely focused on protecting the evidence. It was all I could do not to throw up. At some point the prisoners were escorted back to their cells, the whole jail put into lockdown. I don't really remember when. The bigger picture is a blur. At one stage, I saw Debra's body being carried out. She was alive, but only just. I felt nothing. This was the only murder to ever be committed inside a women's jail in Australia. It was violent, it was ugly and it was gruesome. And I saw the whole thing.

Chapter 1

Early life

*Children should be seen, then
have the crap belted out of them*

My mother once said I should have been drowned at birth. I sometimes wonder why she didn't do it. In all of my life I don't ever remember her saying that she loved me. In fact, far from it. Violence peppered my childhood, the one constant in an ever-changing sea of faces, buildings and people. There were good times, of course, but they were always short-lived and accompanied by the fear of what would come next. People say that you learn a lot from your parents, and if that's true, I learnt about violence.

When I was two years old, we lived in a hostel in East London. It was called Bromley House. Carol, my brother, Michael, my mother and I were all crammed into one room. When I was four, we moved upstairs into a two-bedroom flat. We were all squashed into this tiny space, with nowhere to hide and nowhere to call our own, so these were not happy times for us children. My younger sister Carol and I took the brunt of our mother's anger, the slaps, kicks, smacks and glares, passed down to us like a family heirloom. Our father was not in the picture, although at this point, we were none the wiser. We assumed our mother's partner, Bob the Sailor, was our dad. I didn't realise until I was thirteen that this was untrue, but that's a story for later on.

It's fair to say that I grew up in poverty. We had no bathroom and only a toilet on the outside of the apartment, connected to the kitchenette. We would have a bath once a week in a big metal tub in front of the fire. The smell of Spam sizzling on the stove would linger in the flat, cloying in the air, and drive me retching into the bedroom. To this day I still can't go near the stuff. Littering the fireplace were dirty cigarette butts, which Carol and I once tried to smoke. Left to our own devices, we were two kids under five, puffing away on these little stubs, coughing our lungs up. Our mother heard us spluttering away and shouted through the door, demanding to know what we were up to. We quickly put them out, calling 'Nothing!' We didn't know if this would warrant a beating, but we could make a pretty good guess.

We soon moved into a three-bedroom townhouse in Battersea, along with Bob the Sailor. This is where my sister Cindy was born, in 1962. It was right next to the train station and a small park where we would escape and play for hours on end. We even had a little balcony. Carol and I would climb up onto a long line of garages next to the station, running wild with the other children. We would be jumping across the train lines, dodging the rails in a whirlwind of restless energy. We knew the tracks were electric, but this just fuelled our games, creating excitement in our desperate lives. I've always been a risk taker – in relationships, jobs, big decisions. But at this time I didn't know that's what I was doing; it was just the thrill. Pushing boundaries and breaking rules, with no one there to stop me.

But playing often turned into fighting. Knocks on the door from the neighbours informing my mother that I'd hurt their sons weren't out of the ordinary. I would scrap with anyone, but especially the boys. Unfortunately, Carol would end up on the receiving end too. I knew I would be punished but I just carried on. Of course, this just increased my beatings at home. At least it gave my mother a real reason to hit me. It made sense and gave an explanation to my punishments. She started with just her hand, but then it became too bruised. She moved on to anything she could find: a hairbrush, a stair rod, whatever was within closest reach. The belt really hurt.

But the worst was when we didn't know it was coming. One evening I was standing next to the stove watching her cook. She suddenly whizzed around and slapped me right across the face. The shock seared my skin and I stumbled. 'What was that for?' I asked. She shrugged. 'Just in case,' she said. This was not unusual. We would be standing in front of her and a certain look would pass over her face. 'Come closer,' she'd say. I'd obey and edge forwards a little. 'Closer,' she'd order. This would continue, a daring dance until I was within reaching distance, where she'd whip out a hand and smack me across the face, a hot burst of energy across my skin. It had always been like this and I didn't know anything else.

It wasn't just at home in secret either. She'd suddenly snap in the shops or the street. People would stop and stare, but I don't ever remember anyone offering to help us. As I got older it only got worse. Once, after a particularly bad beating, Carol was sent upstairs to our room to check if I was still alive. Another time, as we were leaving for school, she slammed Carol's foot in the door, crushing it badly, grinding the bones against the frame. On the way to the hospital our mother warned Carol not to tell the doctors how she did it. And, of course, she didn't say a word.

Aside from the physical violence, my mother was a cold woman. However, we knew that before she went to bed, she would come in to check on us. So we would purposely sleep without our blankets pulled up, hoping she would come and tuck us in. Sometimes this worked, her guard dropping as she cocooned us into a temporary sanctuary. This was the only thing she did that made us feel cared for and special. I still wonder why she could only show kindness towards us when we were unconscious. It was like she couldn't bear the thought of us thinking she loved us. It wasn't uncommon to be sent to bed with no dinner. We'd have to sneak downstairs to make a jam sandwich, scuttling away before we were caught. Looking back, I'd always envy other children's lives – going home to a house with caring parents, where someone gave a real shit about them.

Living like this I learnt how to watch people, to manipulate the situation so I could survive. From the outside I was such a prim, proper child. People saw this sweet little girl and thought butter wouldn't melt in my mouth. I suppose I had to use this to my advantage. I certainly still do it if I need to.

My mother actually once tried to give me away. It was just after Michael was born, in 1958. Michael is my half-brother, Bob the Sailor's son. An American couple would arrive and take me on trips in their car. I don't recall too much, except the rumble of the car's engine, deep

From left: Carol, Michael and me when my mother was going to give me away

and reverberating. One day they arrived to take me, but I refused to leave, crying and hiding behind Bob. He sent them away and I didn't see them again. Years later, my mother told me they were friends of the people who ran the hostel we lived in. I sometimes wonder how different my life would have been if they'd taken me with them.

Chapter 2

Bob the Sailor

The Claytons dad

The day I found out that Bob the Sailor was not my real father was surprisingly normal. There was no grand reveal, no emotional confession, not even a scandalous cover-up. I was thirteen years old, living in Battersea, and was snooping around the kitchen, looking for something or other. Now, I was a curious child, that's for sure, but this was not what I had expected to find. It was paperwork for a court application requesting access to see me from Frederic Bradbury. Frederic Bradbury. This meant absolutely nothing to me. Apart from the fact that my mother was Sylvia Bradbury.

Naturally, I was devastated. My life hadn't been easy, but I'd at least had two parents. Or so I thought. I knew my mother was a liar, but this was something else. I mean, we called him 'Dad'. Looking back now this was one of many in a long list of deceits I encountered growing up, but at the time it made a huge impact on me. It created a sense of even more turbulence in what was already an unstable childhood. I knew that the houses and places we lived in would change, but I hadn't realised the people would as well. It was as if in a split second my whole perception of my family had shifted.

I ran to tell Carol immediately. We then told Michael. We took him into the bedroom and sat him down. However, we didn't tell Cindy. Even at that age I knew she was too young to understand, and it would only hurt her. I can't remember if I realised that Michael and Cindy were Bob the Sailor's children at this point. But in hindsight there were moments that suddenly made a lot more sense to me. I remember sitting around the kitchen table years ago with all of my siblings and my mother. I asked her, 'Why do Cindy and Michael always get things from Dad but not me and Carol?' Of course, she didn't tell me why. She just brushed me off with some flippant comment. Or perhaps completely ignored me. Or flew into a rage. I can't quite remember. But I know for certain that if I hadn't found that piece of paper, then she would never have told me. To this day I would still think Bob was my father. Now, maybe one of us would have stumbled across something years later, but it certainly wouldn't have come from my mother. She was an unapproachable woman, to say the least.

We used to go to these big Christmas parties at Bob's work. I remember being ten years old and his boss calling out the names of all the children. He shouted 'Susan Metcalfe!' calling me up. It confused me at the time. I knew my surname was Bradbury and had no reason to think that this meant anything. It was just how it was. Bob's colleagues would always use his surname when speaking to us, so I suppose he referred to us as his kids too.

When I look back, I do remember being treated well by Bob. There wasn't too much outright favouritism and I felt equal to my siblings in the obvious ways. But, after the secretive nature of my discovery, the grand reveal of my uncovered knowledge to Bob and my mother was far more dramatic. This happened a little while later. We'd kept our revelation a secret, biding our time to let them know we knew until it was right. I don't know if I did this on purpose or not. But it felt good to have a secret, it felt powerful. It gave me a sense of control.

When the moment finally unfolded, I was standing on the stairs of our house in Battersea, arguing over something or other with Bob. I saw his fist rise, ready to smack me. 'You can't hit me! You're not my dad!' I shouted. He stopped, poised in shock. He lowered his hand, his face a picture of confusion. He turned and walked away, into the lounge where my mother was sitting. She would have heard the whole thing. But she didn't say a word. No one came to ask me how I knew, checked if I was okay. I was left standing there on the stairs, braced for the punch that never came.

Since then I've found out some more of the details about my mysterious father. Born in 1927, he was eight years older than my mother. They were married, but my mother left him when she was pregnant with Carol. He suspected the child may not be his, as he was certain she was having an affair with another man. This other man was in fact Bob the Sailor. My mother says my father hit her once, but that it wasn't a violent relationship. A part of me had thought that it must have been, as it would have explained why she was so violent towards us. They divorced on the grounds of adultery. Back in those days, you needed a reason to end a marriage.

Carol and I tried to research that side of the family a while back. We didn't find much, but we know he lived in London and had another family. I suspect that we have half brothers and sisters out there, but I haven't been in touch. Maybe it's something I'll look into one day. However, we did discover some Swedish and German roots in our father's ancestry. It feels strange to know there's a whole other side of my family that has never been a part of my life.

Back to Bob the Sailor. It turns out he wasn't really a sailor, although he was in the navy at some point. I always knew he'd visited the house because I could smell him. I'd open the front door and be hit with the scent of Old Spice, Brylcreem and rollies. This was before he moved in with us. Once we all moved to Battersea, he became a permanent fixture for a while. I didn't realise at the time, but he actually had another family. I'm not sure if my mother knew this either, although it wouldn't surprise me. He somehow managed to keep seeing them and hide them from us. Apart from Carol. One afternoon, when she was about eleven years old, he took her out to meet them. She had no idea who they were, and I wonder if they knew who she was. It wasn't until years later we found out. I still wonder to this day what he was thinking.

Bob and my mother were together on and off for around five years. I'm not sure if you could call it a happy relationship but it lasted, that's for sure. Even once they'd split up, he still came back every Thursday to visit us. He'd bring a bar of chocolate for us children and then hand over the money for rent and food to my mother. He was a better dad to me than my birth father, although I suppose that wasn't very hard. The day they broke up was volatile. I heard them arguing in the bedroom, shouting and yelling at each other. The door banged open and Bob stormed out, his belongings hastily stuffed into a bag, his life with us so quickly packed up. I soon learnt that he had left my mother for one of our neighbours. I shouldn't have been surprised about this really.

The real drama didn't unfold within the confines of our house. It happened in the street outside, as our whole neighbourhood gathered to bear witness to our chaotic family. I was inside when I heard the commotion. I went out into the road to find my mother, Carol, Michael and Cindy standing outside a house a couple of doors down. My mother was yelling. It turned out that Bob had left my mother for a woman who lived almost next door, Anne. I didn't know much about her. However, she was married, and her husband and sons were not happy about it one bit. This was when things escalated. I've already mentioned before that I was a fighter. A feeling would just rise up inside me and I'd turn, hitting or grabbing whoever it was that I knew needed putting in their place. I've always felt powerful when I'm fighting someone, and this moment was one of those.

Anne's sons were livid. They were shouting at my mother, at my siblings and at me, 'You've taken our mother away from us!' Anne's eldest son was looming in front of me, his angry face full of rage. This was when I took a swipe at him, smacking him across the face, hard. My mother tried to hold me back. Well, she tried to make it look like she did, but there was little conviction. I think deep down she was enjoying it. She thought he deserved it. Despite her meagre efforts I persevered, the heat travelling through me, my body brimming with adrenaline. Fighting gave me something that I couldn't quite name, but I loved it. After I'd hit him, my mother did become angry. She started yelling, 'This is a matter between us!' Looking back, I can see that we didn't need to all get involved. But at the time it was just what I did. This was the beginning of the end of Bob and my mother's relationship. He would flit back into our lives for many more years, even moving across the world to the other side of the planet to try and keep the family together.

Chapter 3

School

First steps in a brilliant academic life

I was twenty-eight when I read my first book. I'm not talking about a long, classic, literary book either, just picking up any book and reading it. At sixteen I still couldn't write or spell. Attempting either would paralyse me with fear. I'd become overwhelmed with feelings of shame, guilt and anger. I now know that I'm dyslexic, but for years I had no explanation for my inability to complete the simplest tasks, tasks that everyone else was able to do so easily. The letters would swim on the paper in front of me, jumbled up in a mess of garbled lines and marks. It was like there was this secret that everyone else knew except me. I didn't understand why it was so difficult, why my brain wasn't working. I felt stupid and alone. I didn't learn how to write properly, all the capital letters in the right places, until the early nineties.

School was not a happy place. My first school was called Christ Church Primary School, and I hated it. I was disruptive in the classroom and still picking fights outside. I couldn't keep up with the other kids and this filled me with shame, provoking my feelings of inadequacy and enhancing my wild tendencies. I had fought every single boy in my class, channelling my frustrations into something I was good at: violence. Of course, it wasn't obvious to me at the time that this was a response to my lack of progress in class. Like many children, I just thought that I hated school. I sat in the back left corner of the classroom, not by choice but because that's where the teacher decided I belonged. Tucked out of the way. Maybe they thought I would just melt into the background, become occupied with staring out of the window, and they could turn a blind eye because I was 'unteachable'. But I've always been fiery and before long I was exiled to a solitary desk outside the headmaster's office. Separated from the other children, I felt even more isolated. I'd spend the mornings there and then go to another school in the afternoons. This other school was meant to teach me to read and write but I absolutely hated going there. It was no different to my normal class and simply added to the crushing weight and realisation that I was hopeless. I felt I would never be as good as the other kids.

The best thing about primary school was the food. Every lunchtime we ate a hot meal, without fail. This was very different to my life at home. Although, there was one incident with a spotted dick pudding. I have always had a hatred of dried fruit, and still do to this day. The dinner ladies forced me to eat the pudding, but I refused. They even went and called the headmaster to try and help. Now, I can't see why anyone cared that much – perhaps it was an attempt at controlling me, calming my unruly behaviour. But I was having absolutely none of it. I wouldn't even let them put the spoon near my mouth, wedging my lips firmly shut.

Secondary school was no different, although I did eventually learn to read. I must have been around twelve or thirteen. All that time sitting outside the headmaster's office had left me with a lot of holes in my education. I was behind in class. The mixed school had refused to take me, due to my continued aggression towards the boys. So instead I went to Garratt Green comprehensive, an all-girls school with tennis courts and a swimming pool. A lot of the girls at my school were Jamaicans from Brixton and they'd play reggae music when we went to the gym. We'd dance and move and sway; I'd feel free in those moments. These were some of my happy memories from school.

Unlike at primary school, I was not so disruptive in the classroom at Garratt Green. Maybe I'd accepted I was never going to be top of the class. In fact, I was at the bottom, in the lowest grade possible. But learning to read was a game changer. It was my English teacher who invested in me. It took a long time, but once it began to work it was like a whole new world had been opened up. It would take many years for me to truly feel comfortable reading, but being shown a slither of this secret that had eluded me for so long was profound. Because I was in the bottom grade, we were only taught the most basic classes. All of these kids, many of us who just needed extra support, were written off, discarded as troublesome or stupid. There could have been so much talent hidden there under these chaotic home lives, concentration issues and undiagnosed learning difficulties.

I did once push a girl down the stairs. She'd slapped me around the face during a swimming class, completely unprovoked. She was much bigger than me and I knew that retaliating in that moment would have ended badly. I was seething, my face and pride raw and radiating an electric heat. Later on that day, walking behind her, I saw my opportunity. I didn't feel bad at all. After all, she'd hit me first, so she deserved it. I still didn't realise that violence shouldn't be the first response. But at least she didn't slap me again.

There were things I did enjoy though. It was always the creative things. We had cooking lessons, making food from complete scratch. In textiles we learnt to sew, how to make clothes. It was the practical things that I loved. The feeling of being able to create something all by myself built my confidence, grew my independence. I even remember my clothes being worn in a school fashion show; I was so proud.

At my school each year group had a different colour uniform. Mine was bright turquoise and I absolutely loved it, this joyful conformity. We still wrote with ink pens back then and we had these little pots in the corner of our desks, filled with midnight blue. We also had a typing class. I adored using the typewriters – clack clack, clackety clack. I was fast, a lot faster than most of my classmates. But the speed of my fingers couldn't compensate for the spelling. My sentences were littered with out of place capital letters, phonetically rehashed words, untranslatable utterances. Thinking back, it pains me even now.

My desk was an absolute jackpot, right next to the window and the radiator. We were seated in alphabetical order, so I guess this was one good thing that my father passed down to me. I would gaze out of the window during lessons, my eyes wandering across the field to the large building opposite. It was the Springfield University Psychiatric Hospital. The patients would often be out in the large gardens, meandering through their lives. Deep in conversation with themselves, carefully orchestrating some unknown ritual, quietly interrogating their days away. I saw some strange things from that classroom. And a lot of completely normal things. It introduced me to the sorts of places I would end up frequenting more often than I'd like to.

Despite my difficulties, I only ever skipped school once. Like I've said before, I was a curious child and the experiences that school provided for me beat anything else I could entertain myself with. That's not to say the fear of a beating from my mother didn't also play a part in this. During my time at secondary school I suffered from severe acne, spots crowding my face, amassing in a painful convergence. It hurt so much that sometimes I'd have to stay home, a cold towel delicately placed on my face, attempting to soothe the battle on my skin. Eventually I began getting steroid injections to ease the inflammation. I finally left school aged fifteen in September 1970. I was excited about what was next, but my unexpected motherhood was a surprise.

Chapter 4

Max

A marriage made in hell

I often wonder if I should have killed Max. Of course, I would have been punished. There's no way I'd have been able to cover up a crime like that. He took so much from me, from our children, from our lives. He damaged us all with his violence and controlling manipulation, his selfishness and cruelty. He tainted even my few fond memories of our relationship with ripples of pain, an evil undertow pulling at everything I had. Of course, it didn't start out that way. It wasn't bad at the beginning, right at the beginning when we first met. But we were kids then. In fact, I used to smack him. Not in an abusive way, but we would tussle, play fighting, wrestling. But I never wanted to hurt him, not in the way it seemed he wanted to hurt me.

I was just twelve years old when

Max and me still in school

Max and I first met. His family were from Bangladesh and ran a restaurant in Dulwich. His father had been in the army, serving in Burma, so had a British passport, which he'd used to travel over to London with Max and his older brother. Max's mother and sister stayed in Bangladesh until they saved up enough to come and join them. They were Muslim but his father was a keen gin drinker. We would play out in the street, Max, another boy called Maxwell and me. He was thirteen and his dad would give him pocket money. This was unbelievable to me, the idea of a parent having extra money to give away to their child, to allow them to spend it on whatever they wanted. I suppose this was one of the reasons I carried on hanging out with him. He would pay for Maxwell and me to go to the cinema or the swimming pool. I could never have afforded this without him. However, my mother was livid about my new-found friend. A beating would ensue every time she caught me hanging around with him. Perhaps she had a bad feeling, a mother's intuition. Or perhaps it was just another reason to beat the shit out of me. Either way, it didn't work.

We carried on this way for years, just being friends. It wasn't until I was fifteen or so that it developed into something else. Now, I would never describe our relationship as romantic – that would be going too far. I certainly never loved him. But he gave me the attention that I craved. At home I was still unloved, rejected, ignored, so when he would follow me about, wanted to spend time with me, to talk to me and be with me, I would jump at the chance. I did have other friends outside of this little trio, but not ones I could confide in. I know that if I had had more of a support system, I might have thought twice about getting involved with Max.

I was fifteen when I became pregnant. There wasn't any world in which I expected this to happen. It didn't cross my mind that this was a possibility, which just shows how naive I was. I didn't tell my mother, but somehow she knew. I suppose she saw the signs – the sickness, the flush of my cheeks, my slowly changing body. One afternoon she came into my room and announced we had to go to catch the bus. I was unsure what was happening, but I followed meekly, as I knew I had to. Maybe we were going to the shops, or maybe we were going into town together. It turned out we were going to the hospital. She told me I had an appointment with the doctor, so I went in, completely oblivious to what was about to happen.

There were three men sitting in front of me, their eyes needling my body. Their cold faces stared at me, a scrawny, malnourished teenager with inflamed skin and an aura of fear. I must have looked so young, so weak. 'You've come for an abortion?' they asked. A wash of heat spread through me, electrifying my fingers, sharpening my mind. 'No,' I said coolly. And that was that. I turned around and left the room. My senses were overwhelmed, sounds got louder, every noise pummelling at my eardrums. The bright lights blistered my retinas, scorching my vision with a tangled array of colours. I felt light-headed, shocked at what had just happened but not surprised at all.

As I rejoined my mother in the waiting room, the world did not slip back into focus. She sat there, waiting patiently and seemed bored, as if it was just another mundane afternoon. She turned her head towards me. 'Did you make the appointment?' she asked. I told her what I'd told the doctors. She looked at me carefully, slowly. I met her gaze, locking eyes with her, holding her stare. I don't know who broke away first. But it wasn't a big moment. There was no scene, no dramatic argument, no discussion. We left the hospital and caught the next bus home. On the bus, I stared out the window, watching the condensation dribble down the scratched glass, the outside world a hazy blur.

We were sitting on the top deck, on the left-hand side. My mind was frantic, but I remember that day with such clarity. The traffic was loud, and the vibrating bus wobbled. I glanced at my stomach, at what it was now, a vessel for something unfathomable. My mother turned to me and said, 'When we get home, pack your things and get out.' I looked at her. Her face was even, not a shred of emotion. She turned away and we carried on in silence. When we arrived home, I packed my things and left.

It was cold outside, very cold. I tramped down the dirty streets, my bag trailing behind me in the tarmac gloom towards Battersea Power Station on Circus Road. I didn't really have any choice about where I could go. It was only Max. He was staying with his uncle in rented rooms and he put me up in one of them. Bob the Sailor worked in the same street at the Battersea Power Station, but I didn't see him during that time. This was the beginning of a dark period of my life, a period I don't wish to forget but I would never return to. It still makes my belly ache, my brain fog over just to think about it. I'd rather forget, but I know I can't.

By that time, I had already left school and was working in the Royal Marsden Hospital in their records department. It was 1970 and my neighbour had helped me get the job. It was over in Chelsea, a specialist cancer treatment hospital. My job was to collect the patients' records, put them in alphabetical order and then file them away. However, although school had helped me with the basics of reading and writing, I still didn't know my alphabet. The records would often go missing or disappear altogether in this storm of frantically filed papers, shoved into what I hoped was the right drawer or box. This only added more shame to my ever-growing collection. In the evenings, once I'd finished causing chaos in the hospital, I'd wind my way across London to the East End. Here, I worked a second job as a sewing machinist with Max, stitching coats together piece by piece.

I had realised I was pregnant in November 1970. I'd been out of school for two months, had had one month in the workplace, playing at being an adult. I was frightened and confused, wondering what was going to happen to me and my baby. I don't think I'd even properly considered that from now on it would always be me and my baby.

The night my mother kicked me out, when I finally reached Max's uncle's flat, I was exhausted. The place was cold and empty. It felt like no one had lived there for a long time, never made it their home. I was alone a lot. Max was still out working at the sewing factory, so I was left with little to do to pass the time. Hunger consumed my days. Without the blanket of those hot school dinners, without my absent but nevertheless providing mother and siblings, I was slowly starving. I would wake up with my stomach in knots, the raw ache of emptiness contradicting its now painfully evident swell.

One day I got so desperate I clambered out and went down to the shops, planning to steal some food. I was desperate to eat. But even in this time of absolute turmoil, I couldn't do it. Was it fear? Was it shame? Or was it a sense of righteousness? To this day I'm not quite sure. I tried the red phone box outside in the street, seeing if I could break into the cash box and slip a few coins. This felt more detached, less like I was stealing from a real person. But I couldn't manage this either. Leaving home taught me a lot of things about myself, including that I'm a terrible thief.

Days and weeks slipped past me in a haze. I drifted in and out of sleep, too hungry and exhausted to do anything. My body was weak and my mind was without hope, the small dribbles of light that I'd once had spilling into empty puddles. I was certainly depressed, anxious and alone. Max came and went, returning from work to sleep and leaving again early in the mornings. I didn't know what to do.

But then we moved. I'm not sure if we were asked to leave but it was Max who made the decisions. I just followed. When we'd been kids, friends, we'd scrapped with each other all the time. But now, he was very much not my equal anymore. The fighting quickly became one-sided – he'd lash out at me and I'd try to retaliate, but I was tired and malnourished, and I couldn't fight back. Our future was one of violence and abuse, and this was only the first foreshadowing of what would later unfold.

Our next place was a tiny flat in Aldgate with a lady, her husband and their two children. It was a one-bedroom flat, with all six of us crammed in together, stacked on top of each other like bricks in a wall. Max and I shared a bunk bed with their children. Thinking back, I can't believe they let us stay there with them. But it didn't last long and they soon asked us to leave. I don't blame them. After that we moved down to a flat below, in the same building, with an old man. That didn't last long either.

Shortly after moving to Aldgate, I managed to get a job in an office, sorting files and ordering receipts. This place had a machine that could alphabetise the receipts, so I didn't have the constant worry of getting it wrong, getting caught out. I enjoyed this job, especially when the tea trolley came around. It made me feel like a real person again, not purely defined by my bulbous belly.

There was an older woman who lived in the flat above ours. She probably wasn't that old, but everyone seemed like it back then. I could hear voices upstairs, unfamiliar footsteps and creaks. I went over, curious about what was going on, searching for a distraction from my starving boredom. I pushed open her door, and inside stood two police officers. They turned to me, looked me up and down, and clocked my swollen abdomen. A sneer of distaste wrapped around the tallest one's fleshy jaw. They told me she had been broken into.

I traipsed back downstairs, a strange feeling of restless anxiety building inside me. I didn't like the way that policeman had been looking at me. That evening, I heard a bang on the door. It was the police – not the same officers I'd met earlier but this time a man and a woman. They told Max and me that we had to come with them to the station. I was confused and tired, so I followed them meekly. Once we arrived, I was sitting in a cold, bare room, the plastic chair scraping along the floor every time I squirmed in my seat. First a police woman came and spoke to me, but I can't remember what she said. My memories of those months are watery, diluted by the constraints of my tired body.

Then a male policeman came into the room. He wasn't the same man I'd seen in the neighbour's flat, but he carried the same look on his face. I knew straight away this wasn't going to end well. 'Was it worth getting pregnant?' he spat at me, his face a cloud of disgust. I flushed bright red, my cheeks burning in shock and shame. I knew my situation wasn't respectable, but to have strangers speak to me with such hatred hurt. Cruelty oozed from him, while he condemned the choices I'd made. I could tell he thought I was nothing.

They ascertained that I was only fifteen and took my statement. They went around to my mother to tell her where I was living and that legally I wasn't allowed to be living without a guardian. Unsurprisingly, she didn't care. It was then that I realised I wouldn't be going back to the flat. They brought me to another room where a doctor checked me over. I felt like an object, being passed around from person to person, prodded, examined and then moved along. My next destination was a children's home in Poplar.

I was frightened when I first arrived, but I thought it would be safer than living with Max and whichever random families we could persuade to take us in that week. Though it was a children's home, I had to pay rent. I managed to keep working at my job in the office for a good while, until one morning I fainted on the bus on my way in. A passing stranger asked me if I was drunk. Each day I would still go and wait in the queue at the bus stop, but a rising sense of anxiety would burn from within and as soon as the bus arrived, I'd take a step back. I suppose this was the start of my quiet withdrawal from my own life. The raging sense of self was slowly chipped away, and as my body continued to grow, I began to shrink.

The children's home was not a happy place either. I had absolutely no control over what was happening and the home had complete oversight. I would play with the younger children, giving them piggybacks and teaching them how to skip. The staff did not approve of that at all. Perhaps they thought I would lead them astray, or perhaps they didn't like the idea of a pregnant girl being accepted by the group. Either way, they did their best to separate me from the others. One evening, I stayed out all night. When I returned, they were livid. I was taken to a padded room, led in and then the door was locked tightly behind me. I was confused, utterly out of control in all aspects of my life. I couldn't leave when I wanted, I couldn't work, even though I badly wanted to again, and I had no autonomy over even my own body.

I like to think that the staff were looking out for me though, even if I couldn't really see it at the time. They were worried that Max was taking my money to spend on his own selfish needs. This was completely true, but I didn't have the energy to fight him on it. So, one of the women working with me bought me a new bra. She urged me to hide my money there, so he couldn't take it. They weren't happy when I quit my job. I suppose they thought it was good for me to be out and keeping busy, earning a wage and contributing to society. Also, it meant I could pay the rent for my room, which I'm sure they were pleased about.

My pregnancy still amazed me. One morning I realised that my clothes had suddenly become far too short, my bump dragging the hemlines way up. A woman took me to buy some new clothes that would actually fit. We went to Mothercare and returned with one pink and one blue dress. This was all I owned now. As I said, I hated living at the home. I wished I could escape, although I wasn't sure where to. The idea of living with Max again filled me with worry, and my mother's place was not an option.

I found out years later that Bob had been asking about me. He pestered my mother to tell him where I was, who I was with, but she fended him off breezily, papering over the unsavoury details of my deportation. It hurts me to remember that he was not allowed to see me. As he wasn't my birth father, he was unable to visit or contact me. My heart aches a little when I think of this. Knowing that he was looking and cared enough to track me down would have been a spark of happiness in the isolated loneliness that I was living in. I believe he would have taken me to his sister, Gladys, where I would have been looked after.

I'd been in the home for a few months when I realised there was a way out. I was deeply unhappy there and the thought of staying until I was eighteen years old filled me with dread. All I

Max and me on our wedding day, 15 May 1971

Cutting the wedding cake in the children's home, 1971

had to do was get married. I was already bringing so much shame to everyone I encountered, treated with disgust, cast around like an unwanted gift. Maybe this would bring me stability. Maybe it would make Max treat me right, how a wife should be treated. I decided this was the best option.

Looking back now, I can see that it was not. But the care homes wanted to get rid of

Our wedding, outside the registery office, 15 May 1971

children whenever they could – they were overcrowded and underfunded as it was already. They were good to me on a basic level, but it was still an institution. The system didn't look out for our best interests. I didn't have a social worker or someone professional to talk to. Or anyone I felt I could talk to. I didn't have any real friends, only people I knew through Max. I felt so caught, so trapped.

Unsurprisingly, my mother agreed to the wedding. A married daughter with a child was far preferable to the alternative. However, Max's father did not. We actually went to court to attain the right to get married and I can't quite believe that we won. We were wed on the 15th of May 1971 in a registry office. It was just six weeks after my sixteenth birthday. We held the reception at the children's home. It must have been a strange sight, a child bride dressed in a pink Mothercare pregnancy dress and hordes of kids running around. More like a children's birthday party than a wedding. Only Carol and her friend came to the wedding. I left the children's home that very night.

After the wedding, I moved back in with Max. This time it was a one-bedroom flat in Battersea. I'd hated being at the home, but at least there was food there. Now I was back to the long days of starvation, sleeping and sitting alone in the room with no one to talk to and no way of getting food to eat. Carol dropped by to visit one afternoon and she brought a bag of chips. The hot fat seared my nostrils, my pupils dilating as I inhaled the salty, sour pile of potatoes soaked through with vinegar. She didn't know I hadn't eaten in days and I was too embarrassed to tell her. Even at such low points, such times of need, I couldn't ask for help. The fear of rejection, and lack of belief that someone might actually come to my aid, was unshakable. Instead, I suffered. I'd always been strong-willed and I think getting through those days of my first pregnancy hardened me in a way that was irreversible. I'm sad to say, though, that it wasn't the worst I endured. We soon moved again, this time into a tiny room in Max's friend's mum's house. Shortly after, I went into labour and my life suddenly became someone else's too.

I was in the laundrette when a staggering pain took a hold of me. I gasped, stopping what I was doing, clutching myself. Realising what was beginning to happen, I walked back to the house, to our tiny bedroom, and lay down. I stayed there all night, Max asleep beside me, my eyes wide open, staring at the ceiling as wave after wave of pain rolled through. By the morning, I knew I couldn't ignore it any longer, so I walked from Battersea to Chelsea hospital. It was only thirty minutes, but it took everything I had to get myself there; it felt like hours. Vomit expelled itself from my body, a trail of sad breadcrumbs tracing my journey from home.

Max actually came to meet me at the hospital. He was not a good man, but he did have his moments. However, at this time the doctors sent him away, saying he couldn't be there with me. This hurt a lot. I was in so much pain and just wanted someone to be with me, to tell me it was all right. I was terrified. I had no idea what was going on, slipping in and out of consciousness in this alien place full of strangers. A nurse gave me an enema and tried to get me to take a bath. This was the last thing I wanted to do, as I was still vomiting and passing faeces. Eventually they took me into the labour room. I wanted to curl up and die. I kept trying to lie on my side, but the nurses would push me onto my back again. After hours of excruciating pain, my son was finally born. I named him Jeffery. I asked the nurse to help me spell his name on the birth certificate, but she wouldn't. I don't know if that was what they were told to do or if she just didn't want to help me. Because I wasn't sure how to write it, to this day his name is spelt incorrectly.

Shortly after that Carol took Jeffery around to my mother's in the pram. I was hiding behind the garage watching when my mother answered to door. Carol said, 'I've got Susan's new baby here. Would you like to see him?' I was stunned when my mother said, 'No!' and slammed the door shut.

Chapter 5

Poverty and violence

And pork sausages for the soul

After Jeffery was born, staying in the current house became impossible. We were on the public housing list, but it was taking too long. So, we heard it would be faster if we agreed to move out of London. I didn't have any reason to stay, having been cast out by my mother and with no friends to really speak of. Soon, we were offered a three-bedroom council house in Wellingborough, an hour and a half outside of London by train. We visited it before we moved; it was unfurnished, completely empty. The ground floor was concrete, cold and rough, while upstairs bare floorboards lined the bones of the house. Once we agreed to take it, we went straight to a furniture shop and got a bed, one cupboard and a table and chairs, as well as an old 1950s gas stove. We had to rent them, as we didn't have enough money to buy anything. A sofa was given to me, but it collapsed so I stuffed it up with old clothes. I was very good at making do ... I had to be.

Ours was one of several houses wedged in together in a

circle around a patch of grass in the centre. There was even a garden. I'd never had a garden before, never really had much green space. London was a jigsaw of tarmac and asphalt, cracked pavements and potholes. Here there was an apple tree in the garden, sagging with fruit. I was hopeful for what this change would bring, desperate for something good.

Max at 18 and me at 17

It was the autumn of 1971 when we arrived. I remember sitting in the house, on one of our few chairs, a cold draught blowing through the building. We didn't even have curtains, so I made a pair out of an old sari. They were pretty see-through, but better than nothing. I was sixteen years old, with a newborn baby, living in a small town where I knew nobody. Our neighbours were all almost double my age, so I found it difficult to make friends with them. I was incredibly lonely and scared. I had not really expected Max to be a comfort, but I hadn't anticipated just how bad things would become between us.

I was alone a lot. Max spent much of his time travelling back to London, to work, to see his family and eagerly spiralling into a life of petty crime. He didn't really want the nuclear family, the responsibility of a wife and child. He was only seventeen. I was willing to play at being an adult, mainly because I didn't have another choice, but he was firmly set on living hedonistically in the city.

One afternoon, I heard a knock at the door. I shuffled across the cold floor, Jeffery attached to me at the hip, my face pale. A woman was standing outside. She lived a couple of houses down and told me she wanted to just pop over to see how I was finding the move here. I asked her in, and we chatted a little before she went away. Later that day, there was another knock at the door. This time it was her husband. Like his wife, he came into the house while his eyes flickered around the place. He stayed for a little while, chatting and asking questions about me, Jeffery and Max. I think they wanted to check on me and my living situation. At the time, I thought I needed to hold moments of kindness like that close, for when I forgot there were people out there who were on my side when they really had no reason to be. In fact, they weren't being kind, merely nosey, curious and astonished at my impoverished circumstances. Sad.

After they left, I shuffled back to my chair in the kitchen where the TV balanced on the table as there was nowhere else to put it. I opened the oven. It was on full blast, the heat radiating through the damp air, warming my frozen face. Jeffery was in his pram, sleeping next to me, hidden under bundles of blankets and clothes, layer upon layer.

As I've said before, Max was an abusive husband. And after Jeffery was born, he became an abusive father. He didn't stay at our house in Wellingborough very often, which was a relief. I was lonely but at least when he wasn't there I didn't live in a constant state of fear. When he did stay overnight, he would get angry when Jeffery cried. Max would clamp his hand down over Jeff's mouth and nose, silencing him and cutting off his air until he stopped screaming. This awakened a sense of wild panic within me. I had no doubts that Max would hurt my baby. Max could see how this destroyed me, so would use it against me. He would tell me that if I really wanted him to stop, to let Jeffery be, I had to give him a blow job. And, of course, I did. Going to sleep each night when Max was there, I was terrified for Jeffery, terrified that one day Max would leave his hand over his mouth for too long, and that when he stopped crying, he wouldn't start again.

Max's violence could erupt at any time, unexpectedly and out of nowhere. One night I woke up struggling to breathe, feeling my mouth and nose blocked by an ever-increasing weight over my face. I couldn't scream. I had no breath, kicking wildly and bucking my body, trying to suck air. Slowly I felt myself weaken, my oxygen-starved brain sending sparks spinning towards my smothered eyes. My legs felt like lead as strength seeped away from my body. I was going to die, and all I could think about was Jeffery without a mum. In the distance, I could hear shouting. 'Stop, Max, fucking stop!' Suddenly I could see. Gagging for breath, hauling huge gulps of air, I looked up to see Max, pillow in hand and glaring at me like a demon. His friend was standing next to the bed, eyes wide in shock. I would certainly not be here today if he hadn't been there.

After a few months of living like this, Max's older brother and his wife, Andrea, came to stay with us. They had a daughter called Alma and a son, Jeremy. I loved having Alma, Jeremy and Andrea around. It filled the cavern of the empty house, warming the rooms with their chattering buzz and giving me someone to talk to. Max and his brother Paul were down in London a lot, so I spent the days with Andrea. She was kind.

When they first arrived, I thought their presence might dampen Max's violent temper. However, this turned out not to be the case. If anything, the two brothers only encouraged each other. Andrea's face was a permanent rotation of black eyes, a collar of deep blue, and purple blotches blooming around her neck and across her face. She took all of her husband's anger, but he didn't ever touch Alma or Jeremy. This sounds pathetic, but I was jealous of this. Max was so focused on destroying not only me but our child as well. He was a bluster of rage, popping off at the slightest inconvenience, peppering both me and Jeffery with smacks and blows and grabs. It was simple, really, the more unhappy and out of control Max became, the more he hurt us.

By November, when Jeffery was just three months old, I became pregnant again. By now I was under no illusion that having another child together would repair the damage in our relationship. I don't know if you could even call it a relationship really. I knew it would only get worse from here. We were still always hungry, because the little money that Max brought back to the house would only just cover heating and food. We would always try to make sure the kids had enough, but I would often go to bed empty.

Six months passed like this, all of us just surviving. I was by then, quite heavily pregnant with my second child, Ruby. I was edging down the landing in our house, when Max came out of one of the rooms and thrust his foot towards my belly. He didn't look at me, didn't say anything, didn't even break his stride. I doubled over in pain from the impact, grabbing at my precious stomach with a flash of panic for the person inside me. It was moments like this, of unnecessarily casual cruelty, that hurt the most. I lay on the floor, breathing deeply, trying to calm myself. Heaving my swollen body up, I carried on with my day. We didn't exchange a single word.

In Wellingborough, 1972, with Jeffery and Ruby

Shortly after this incident, I was at the doctor's for a check-up on the baby. The doctor saw the coiled bruise spreading across the front of my bump. He asked what had happened and I replied without emotion that I'd walked into something. I can't even remember what I said. He stared at me, an odd look in his eyes. I could tell he didn't really believe me, but he said nothing else. Just carried on with the check-up and then left, and I went home. I sometimes wish I had reached out to someone, that it might have changed things, but at the time I was paralysed with fear.

Ruby was born on the 10th of August 1972, a baby girl, soft, clean and innocent. I knew that I would do whatever I could to make sure my children were okay, that they were as safe as they could be. I was tired, hungry and emotionally exhausted, living in this perpetual state of fear of violence. By September Max had become more tactful in his beatings. It was just a flurry of rage ignited by a tiny spark that would cause him to lash out. It was a slow burning, constant flow of aggression, simmering throughout his entire essence.

One late autumn evening I could feel he was going to snap. He'd been sullen and bristled at my every movement. After we'd eaten, I removed myself from the kitchen, hiding myself away in the back room, trying to melt away into walls. But that was never going to work. I heard his footsteps trudging towards me. Jeffery and Ruby were both under two, nestled in my trembling arms. Max pulled off his studded leather belt, the buckle glinting in the harsh light. He thwacked it down over my body, the slash cutting into my flesh. I was clutching Ruby to my chest, shielding her head from the curled strap. I pushed Jeffery behind me, creating a barrier between his father and him. I was frightened but I wasn't weak. I knew that I was better than this, that this man wouldn't have control over me forever. He couldn't. I just needed to figure out how to break out of this prison I'd stumbled into.

The days and nights continued like this. Max would continue to attack me, by this time regularly throwing hot cups of tea over me, seriously scalding me and hurting our children. I would glide along, emotionless and helpless, desperately trying to convince myself that this wouldn't go on forever. It was a difficult time. We were very poor and just looking after the house and children was tough. Money was very tight and came in irregular, sporadic bursts. I never knew if we were going to have enough to eat or to keep the electricity on. I had twelve cloth nappies between two children and no washing machine. We couldn't afford one. It was the 1970s but the way we were living could easily have been mistaken for Victorian times. I had a galvanised bucket that I would fill with freezing cold water and heave onto the cooker. I'd have to boil the nappies, almost every day, and then dry them out on the washing line to be used again straight after. When it was winter, they'd freeze solid and I'd have to crush the ice and melt their stiffened forms before sliding them back onto the children. Sometimes I had nothing to use as nappies and resorted to using tea towels. I handwashed everything we owned for seven years. Everything.

I only had one set of sheets for the bed so when I wanted to wash them, I had to pick a day when I knew I'd be able to dry them properly. They were threadbare and riddled with holes, each patched up carefully, with precision and care. We had so very little that I treasured each thing so much; nothing could be wasted or rejected. I would sweep the floorboards every day, my broom brushing against the rough, exposed wood. There wasn't enough money for proper flooring or carpets, not even a vacuum cleaner. I do remember once I managed to borrow a Hoover from one of the neighbours. The feeling of relief I felt when I vacuumed the room was embarrassingly joyful. The ease with which it turned hours of work into minutes was glorious.

The early days were long and empty but crammed full of the exhaustive domesticity of raising two children. Andrea and Paul would flit in and out of the house over the years, but I never knew when they were coming or going. I craved stability but instead lived with unpredictable boredom, fear and worry. There used to be a show I'd watch on television. God, that television kept me sane. People often say they wouldn't have made it through trauma such as this in their lives without pivotal people there to support them, but I know that this TV was that for me during those first few years. But also, I very nearly didn't get through them at all.

By February 1973 Andrea and her family had moved out and were living in a high-rise flat near Battersea Park, in a unit in the top right-hand corner of the building, on the fifth floor with two bedrooms and a bathroom upstairs. Andrea would help out at the family restaurant and I would stay in the flat looking after my two children, while Max and Paul, regularly travelled to Scotland with friends and secured girls to work in prostitution, earning them money I never saw.

One afternoon Max went out with his friends and didn't return for almost a week. During this time the flat was burgled. The kitchen window downstairs had been smashed in and glass was sprinkled across the floor through which a trail of scuffed footsteps revealed a path straight towards the TV. They took anything that looked vaguely valuable, which in all honesty wasn't much. But it was terrifying. The kids and I were asleep upstairs when it happened. These men silently slipped into the place where we slept unprotected, unaware of their presence. I could barely sleep at all after that. I sat every night by the window, with a weapon in my hands, sometimes a knife, sometimes a saucepan. I waited for them to return, to come back again, but they never did.

We think someone had come looking for Max's brother. I knew that he and my husband were involved in some unsavoury activities. All these trips down to London, the unreliable spurts of money, the shady people who would come and go from the flat. Max was still gone. It had been days since I'd seen him and I had no idea when he would come back. I'd sit by the window, staring across the rooftops, the cold winter sun spreading its watery light over London. Everything felt pale. My thoughts, emotions, body all diluted into a dull haze.

After the robbery the police came around. I heard a light rap at the door, soft and unassuming, certainly not any of Max's friends. As I shuffled across the flat and cracked open the door, one police officer stood there, peering cautiously over the threshold. I hadn't called the police. His eyes flitted across the room, searching for something. He was looking for Max's brother. They hadn't come about the robbery at all. I told him the truth, that I didn't know his whereabouts. I began to cry, tears slipping over my hollow cheeks and dripping onto the hard floor, staining my clothes with little ovals of darkness. The officer looked at the watery trail and asked me, 'Is everything all right here?' 'Yes,' I managed to say, sucking in a thick, musky breath of air and pushing my shoulders back. Everything was not all right at all. But I knew what children's homes were like, and I would not have my kids taken there; after all, I'd only just escaped one myself. And I knew what would happen if Max found out I'd talked to the police about him. It would only make things worse.

Looking back, this is one of those moments where things could have changed. If I'd asked for help.

We were starving. Of course, we were already hungry, but we literally began to starve. Jeffery and Ruby cried at first, but soon became too weak and would just sleep all day. I'd feed them water, coaxing them to drink when they woke up. I had no money to buy any food and I couldn't steal. I also didn't have a key to the flat, so there was no way of leaving without being locked out.

Another knock came to the door. This time it was rough, a series of shaky thuds. I drew in a breath. turned the lock. It was one of Max's friends, with a wild look in his eyes. Barging past me he quickly glanced over the place. 'Where's Max?' He demanded. I knew this man and told him the truth, 'I don't know.' I was close to tears again, the feelings of desperation crawling back into my voice as I told him we had no food and no money to buy any. He turned and looked at me, his eyes sliding over my face, then down over my thin body. It was the first time he'd propositioned me for sex. He said if I slept with him, he'd give us enough money for food for the next few days. I refused. My hopelessness was replaced by a steely anger, a simmering disgust. I was in a bad way, but I was still a fighter. Even in the depths of poverty I would not let this man have power over me, bend to his will, sell my body to him. He gave me the money anyway.

I ran down to the corner shop, buying whatever I could afford. I don't remember what, but it was hastily tossed into a thin plastic bag, all foil and paper and shiny packaging. He stayed in the flat with the kids to let me back in after. I didn't want to leave them with him for long. He came back a few days later with more money for food. He really helped us out. My expectations were so low that it really felt like he was there for us. More than Max ever was anyway.

He eventually returned. Max that is. I heard the key twist in the lock, the clunk of his heavy footsteps shuffling through the door. He met my eyes and then turned, dragging himself straight upstairs to bed. He just slept. No questions about how we'd survived without him. He didn't even look at the kids. None of this was a surprise to me but it still hurt.

Max would sometimes bring his friends around. This is what I hated the most, because he would always treat me worse. He seemed to enjoy the performance, wanting to show that I was a good, compliant wife, with the sole purpose of living in servitude to him. The problem was that I was not. And perhaps this was why he enjoyed it so much. I would always refuse his requests and then he would batter me until I had no choice but to indulge them or end up unconscious on the floor. It was always fifty–fifty on which way it would go.

One particular occasion still plagues me even today. He had a friend round and asked me to cook them a meal. I cooked for them, placing their plates down on the table. Max bolted up from his chair, smacking his hand across my face. There was no controlling his reactions – if he wanted a fight there'd be a fight. He didn't like the way I'd brought the food to them, the way I'd put it down on the table. I retreated into the kitchen, trying to escape the beating I knew was coming. Riled up, he shoved the chair over so it toppled and, pushing through the door, followed me. The kitchen knife rested on the counter, still speckled with chopped onions. In a flash it was in his hands, raised to my neck. Fear burned through me and I ducked. We wrestled, with him snatching at me and stabbing towards my stomach as I forced his hand away. I managed to duck around him, running upstairs to the bathroom and slamming the door shut, pushing the bolt firmly. I stood there breathing heavily, staring at the locked door.

The sound of shattering glass exploded through the pane in the door. Max had thrown a radio through it. Shards of glass scattered across the floor in front of me. Max tried to climb through, the glass tearing at his clothes and hands. When he had wedged himself halfway through, I opened the door, scraping past him and ran into the bedroom, locking the door behind me again. He couldn't get me in there. But Ruby was in a portable cot downstairs, so I knew I'd have to get out soon. I heard Max leave, then return a few minutes later. He was waiting outside the door for me, breathing heavily. I opened it and he burst through, flinging himself at me with a pair of kitchen scissors in his hands. He pinned me down and began whacking me with the scissors. Grabbing my head, he opened the blades. Sharp, jagged snips fell from his fingers, my hair being hacked off in chunks. He knew how much I loved my hair, keeping it long. He decapitated each strand, until it was barely below my throbbing jaw.

When he was finished, he went back downstairs to eat. He didn't say sorry. He never did. He thought it was his right to treat me this way. I was nothing more than an accessory to him, someone to look after him and do as he ordered. I was still just seventeen. After that attack I decided to kill myself.

Back in the Wellingborough house, Max and I had another argument and, as always, he became violent. But this time it was different. A part of me shifted. I just couldn't bear to live like this anymore, so I went upstairs, locked myself in the bathroom and overdosed. He was bashing on the door, unaware of what I was doing, just desperate to batter my permanently bruised body some more. His friends were downstairs, waiting. The door cracked, splintering down the middle and he crashed in, raising his fists and laying into me. That's the last thing I remember.

I woke up later in a hospital bed. His friends had loaded me into their car, rolled me onto the back seat. Apparently, I'd fallen off onto the floor and so had been driven to the emergency services like a suitcase, wheeled into the waiting room and carted off to the ward. The doctor wanted to send me to another hospital, a psychiatric ward. At least that's what I thought at the time. But Max didn't want me to go. He told me we were leaving. So we did. I discharged myself and we left. That was it.

I don't know how long I was in the hospital, but when we arrived back at the house, I was shocked. It was full of strange men and women. It took me a few moments to realise what was going on. Over the last few months, Max and his friends had been taking trips up to Scotland. All the time he'd spent in London, he'd been pimping. They would drive up north and convince these women to come down to London with them. In Scotland, they'd treat them like they were their girlfriends, like they were in love with them. Promising them a better life down south, they'd convince these girls to come with them. Of course, once they arrived in London the men would explain that times were tough, that they needed to earn some money to survive. The girls were either infatuated or just so starved of attention that they would do anything these men asked. Before long they would slip into a routine of full-time prostitution, handing over the money straight to Max and his friends. The men would spend their days lounging in cafes on Shaftesbury Avenue, while their women went out to sell themselves in the West End.

I knew this had been going on, but I hadn't expected them to be in my house right at that time. One girl was cooking, another was washing up, another had changed the way the curtains hung. I was disoriented and confused, but I just carried on, like I always did. Max introduced them as the girlfriends of each of his friends, but I understood what was happening. Speaking to the women, I was always honest. I tried to warn them, tell them what was in store once they arrived in London. Some of them believed me, some didn't. A few managed to escape once they arrived and I like to think they found a better life. I knew that my loose tongue made Max angry, but I couldn't let them tumble into a life of abuse and control. I was scared of Max, but I had my beliefs and they were strong.

Despite Max's backstreet business, I never saw any more of the money. From then onwards he would disappear for months, to reappear with a bunch of new women later on. We were still dirt poor. It was around this time that Ruby began walking. She'd outgrown her cot, but we had no other bed for her to sleep in. I remember taking the spare double bed and just cutting it in half, sawing sideways down the middle to create two smaller beds. I sewed an old blanket over the gaping hole and nailed on new legs. One for Jeffery and one for Ruby.

It wasn't just a new bed that we couldn't afford. When the time came later on, the children's school shoes were bought in instalments. A man would come every Friday night and collect a little bit of money. I'm sure we ended up paying far more than they were worth, but it was the only way I could afford them. My own shoes had so many holes in them that I used to wear plastic bags over my stockings, in an attempt to keep my feet dry. I only had two sets of clothes myself. One day one of Max's friends came over with a huge sack of old clothes from his ex-girlfriend. I remember rifling through the bag, poring over everything carefully. I'd never had such a choice before; it felt liberating.

Though I had no control over most of what went on in my life at this point, I still had some small rebellions. Later, when the children were old enough to go, we had to notify the school of any food preferences or allergies. I just left the form blank; any food would be welcome and we could not afford to let them be picky. Max asked about this later on, demanding to know if I'd remembered to put down that they were Muslim. I said yes, but of course the answer was no. Max himself did not abide by the rules of Islam: he drank, smoked, gambled and pimped. Sometimes, I'd cook bacon in a frying pan, the fatty, salty smell permeating the house. We couldn't afford it often, so it was always a treat. One morning, I hadn't seen Max in weeks so I thought the coast would be clear. But I heard his key scratching at the lock. Thinking quickly, I shoved the pan, still searingly hot, full of sizzling meat, under the sink. He walked in, throwing a disgusted look my way. He had to have smelt what I was doing, but this time he chose to ignore it, to ignore me, and sighing, he went straight upstairs. I saw no problem in deceiving him. I was not going to let him control our children's lives if I could possibly help it.

Pork sausages were cheaper than beef and nutritious but, being Muslim, Max insisted on the more expensive beef ones. One day, the devil in me served him pork sausages without a mention of what they were. He took his first bite, sighed happily and chewed on with enthusiasm. Watching a line of pork fat dribble down his chin gave me a peculiar sense of satisfaction. From that day on, Max enjoyed pork sausages. Yes, I suppose doing that was malicious, but these small invisible acts of defiance kept me going during those difficult times.

Every week a policeman would come around on his bike. I'd hear the ding of the bell and the clack of the gears as he wheeled it to the door. I'd always invite him in, pour him a cup of tea and we'd chat. He'd ask me about Max, the kids, what was going on. I liked him. I suspect he was officially keeping an eye on Max's dealings, but I like to think he was also keeping an eye on me.

There were also times the police came around and were less friendly. Admittedly, it was because I'd been stealing from our electricity meter. I'd break into the box, pilfering a few coins away to buy food for Jeffery and Ruby. I knew it was wrong, but we were just so hungry. When the electricity meter reader came around, he noticed the box had been damaged, but didn't say anything, just glancing over at the house and leaving. A few days later the police came and took me down to the station. My stomach was in knots, a swirling mass of hunger and fear. I really thought this was the moment they were going to take my children away and throw me into a cell. But they didn't. I was honest and told them that I'd taken it to feed my kids. They looked at me long and hard, before telling me that there would be no further action. I was shocked. They even drove me back home afterwards. There were a few moments of this unexpected and unbelievably touching kindness back in those days that stayed with me a long time.

A couple of years passed this way – an ocean of beatings, hunger and lonely existence. But 1974 brought a change. For a start, Max was sent to jail. The years of backstreet deals, fiddling the law and theft had finally caught up with him. Although, the crime he was sentenced for was the most fitting. For years I had taken the brunt of his beatings, his volatile temperament. But it turned out that this time he'd transferred that anger onto someone else. Max was arrested for grievous bodily harm, committed in the East End, and he was sentenced in the Old Bailey for eight months.

But there was not this sense of freedom, of joy that I was safe from my abuser. Instead, I would go and visit him every week. I'd get the long train into London, then walk across the city to the prison to see him. It took a whole day, but I didn't know what else to do. I would bring the children as well, Jefferey's tiny hands clutched tightly around mine, so alien in this world of bars and alarms. Max's chaotic world mystified me. I heard talk of his friends planning to rob a bank, but no money was ever delivered. I also heard that they stole a chicken from a farm. This seemed far more likely. When he was released, nothing changed. He was not reformed, not a better person. If anything, prison had radicalised him further, supercharged his manic mind. He went straight back to Shaftesbury Avenue, to his friends and his girls.

I spent a lot of time at the kitchen sink. It looked out over the green and the grass where Jeffery and Ruby would play. I would stare out with only one pervading thing running through my mind: 'One day, I'll be free.' A few years back, in 1971, it was here that I heard the news. I found out that my mother was moving to Australia, taking Carol, Michael and Cindy with her. I realised back then that I really was alone, stranded in this small town with no real friends, no family and a violent husband. And although I didn't know it yet, before it got better, it would get worse.

Chapter 6

Jeffery and Ruby

Innocence betrayed

Biju, a relation of Max's mother, thought Jeffery was possessed by the devil. Not in a humorous, spirited, childlike way, but in a full-on, 'we should consider an exorcism' way. As a toddler, he had been completely normal, reaching the expected milestones of any child. But by five years old he had started sleepwalking. We still lived in the council house in Wellingborough and I'd hear him shuffling around in his room. Sometimes I'd hear scrabbling at the back door. I'd creep downstairs, clutching anything I could find to use as a weapon, ready to defend myself against the intruder. But it would be little Jeff, blindly scratching at the door, completely gone to the world. At this point I was worried, but mainly for his safety. While we were in our house, I could keep an eye on him, protect him. But when we stayed overnight in new places, it wasn't so easy.

I was not close with Max's family. In fact, I just tolerated them. His mother thought Max was a blessing on this earth and

Jeffery at 4 years and 2 months

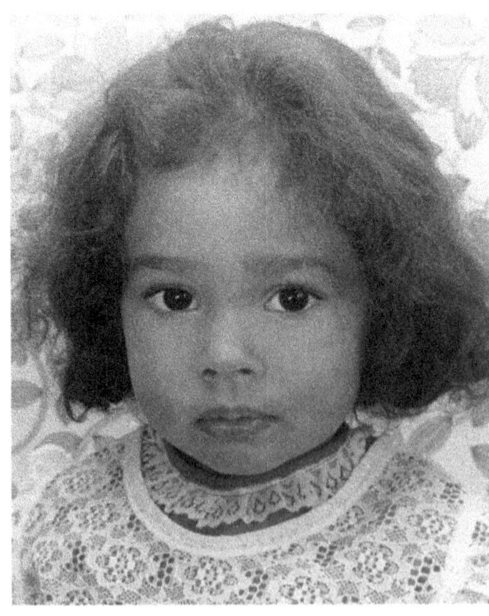

Ruby at 3 years and 2 months

she showed no remorse for his vile treatment of me and our children. She thought it was within Max's duties as husband to discipline his family if they were not satisfying his needs. His father was stern, an outwardly strict Muslim, with a generous splash of alcoholism. He drank gin all day and really thought no one could smell it. He also beat his wife. I did like Max's younger sister, Salma. She was kind to me, helped look after the children. When we went to stay with them in London, Jeffery would climb out onto the balcony at night while he was asleep. We'd find him clawing at the window, trying to edge his legs onto the sill. Max's mother would often sleep in his bed, wrapping her arms around him, trying to stop him from making a move.

He would also talk. The ramblings and mutterings of an unhinged adult would escape his small lips, his brow furrowed and fists clenched. Sometimes it was just whispering, sometimes shouting, ripping through the quiet nights, jolting me awake. Stumbling through the cold hallway, I'd go to him, try to coax him back into bed, soothe his frantic chattering. Sometimes Max would come with me, hanging back by the doorframe. He didn't like to get too close. At first I thought he was just lazy, that he thought this was my job, women's work. But

Me at 18

years later I found out that he was frightened. I have to admit, I was sometimes frightened too. It's an eerie thing to see your child so far away.

One night, familiar crashing and stomps radiated from Jeff's room. I'd gone in to try and calm him down, soothe him into a state of sleep. Pushing open the door, I found his blanket tossed to the floorboards, his pillows thrown across the room. Jeff was pacing ferociously around, knocking into things, bouncing from wall to wall. I led him back to his bed, gently picking up his exiled bedding, and tucked him back in. He woke up with a look of fear and confusion in his eyes. 'Look, Mum. Can't you see him? Can't you see him?' A primal wash of fear slithered up through my shoulder blades, my neck prickling. 'See who, Jeffery?' At moments like this I began to think maybe there was something else going on.

On top of this, he was not doing well at school. Max needed no excuse to torture him, but his academic struggling made him an easy target. He would make little Jeffery stand in front of him and recite the alphabet or his times tables. Words would slip from Jeff's quivering mouth, but they were never the right ones in the right order. A sneer would creep over Max's face as he berated him, carefully picking at his mistakes like at an open wound. Naturally, they did not have a good relationship.

The children knew that they mustn't anger Max. It still hurts me to this day to think how they had to grow up so fast in that respect. I knew what it was like to live in fear of a violent parent. I wish that I'd managed to break the cycle, to shield them from him. But I was barely an adult myself, and despite my efforts, tethering Max when he was in a rage was impossible. As was escaping him.

When they were young, Jeffery and Ruby were close. With only a year between them, they would often play together. A particular favourite game of theirs involved sliding down the stairs on these giant teddies they both had. I would hear the juddering thumps as they skidded down, giggles spluttering from their open faces. But as soon as they heard the key turn in the lock, the teddies would be hastily stowed away, their faces tidied into a solemn, subdued arrangement. Max would walk in and they'd sit quietly, avoiding eye contact, not making a sound. They'd always sit on the floor in the lounge, as Max didn't like it when they sat on the sofa, especially not next to me. He was a possessive man, even though he clearly didn't want me himself. I was another item to collect, another possession that was his and his alone.

I'd managed to get a job in a big department store, working on the cash desk. It meant I had a little bit more money and we were able to eat regularly and feed the power meters. It

heaving. I pulled myself up, shuffling over to Ruby to find her crying on the bed. She was sprinkled with darkening blotches of bruising that were already starting to glow through her pale skin. One of her fingers was bent and she was sniffling into the pillow. I told her to wait up there. I then dusted off my own clothes, squared my shoulders and descended the staircase. Back in the restaurant I sat down at the table feeling sick with anger. Max's mother just looked at me, a blank expression on her face. She would have heard everything that happened up there, as the walls were not thick. But she just turned away and carried on eating.

There were other times she turned a blind eye on her son's brutal behaviour as well, or even worse, encouraged it. There was a small courtyard out behind the restaurant. We were visiting his family and I noticed that Max and Jeffery weren't around. I walked out to find Max towering over Jeffery, laying smack after smack into his small, curled up frame. 'You bastard!' I yelled, dragging Max off him, earning myself a sharp kick and shove to the floor. Max's mother overheard the whole thing and was not happy with how I spoke to him. She thought I deserved a beating for speaking to him in that way.

Max's father wasn't any better. It's strange that as a child I thought of him as a good man, but only because he gave Max pocket money. He was a hypocrite in every way, berating his wife for not keeping the house in order, not living up to his standards. But as I mentioned, he had a tendency for gin and was a selfish man, an unkind alcoholic.

He was fifty-two when he died. Ruby, Jeffery and I had been down for the day to visit him in hospital. He was about to have a brain operation for an aneurism. I didn't like him much but visiting seemed the right thing to do. He seemed fine and at the end of the day we left, getting the train back up to

Wellingborough. Max stayed with him. Around midnight the phone rang. 'He's dead,' uttered Max. 'Oh, okay.' I replied, putting the phone down. I didn't care, didn't feel any sadness. I just went back to sleep.

His body was laid out in a refrigerated drawer in the mosque for people to visit him and pay their respects. Max's family were surprised that I went. And I went more than once. But it wasn't to pay my respects. No, it was to make sure he really was dead, really was gone. Every time I'd see his body, the life fully drained from him, a sense of relief would wash over me. I don't know how many times I opened that drawer to check. Maybe that's a morbid thing to say, but it's true. It confirmed that there really was a way to get rid of an oppressor, that they really could just go. Perhaps a small part of me pretended that this was Max, that this was one step closer to my own oppressor's demise.

Before the funeral, they moved his coffin into the restaurant. Again, it was to give people a chance to pay their respects and say goodbye. But it was a hot day, the usual kitchen heat doubling from the sweaty summer sun and the crowded room. His body wasn't fresh and a stale odour lingered in the restaurant. It was sickly. As he had served in the army, he wanted to be buried in a veterans' graveyard, Brookwood Cemetery, Woking.

We piled into the hearses, crawling away from East Dulwich towards his final resting place. But after a while, the car at the front of the procession pulled over. The others followed suit, like a line of ants trailing in a parade. They had got lost. No one actually knew the way to this graveyard; it was almost comical. Eventually the drivers had to go into a newsagent to ask. It was like something from the *Carry On* movies.

When we finally arrived at the graveyard, it was late, as the time spent circling roundabouts and meandering down unmarked roads had delayed the procession. The cemetery closed at five o'clock and we didn't have long at all. The section he was to be buried in lay right at the bottom of a steep hill from the entrance. We hurried out of the cars, the men grabbing his coffin and shunting him down the hill, their legs whirling. The rest of us stayed at the top. We didn't even walk down the hill, there was just no time. We stood solemnly, watching as his coffin was hastily lowered into the ground, the men sweating in the afternoon sun. They quickly threw the dirt over the grave, piling it on, before tearing away. We made it out just as they came to lock the gates. It sounds like a sad affair and really it was. But I thought it was hilarious.

For a while we had a dog. Well, Max had a dog, I don't remember if we even named it. Even the animal wasn't safe from him. He would beat it so badly it would barely look at him. One afternoon I came home to find it hanging on the coat hooks by the front door. I saw its quivering eyes drooping, its head lolling to one side. Gently unhooking it, I took it down. It crumpled onto the floor, trembling. I wasn't able to set myself or our children free, but I knew I could save this dog. I opened the front door and gave it a light push. It looked at me, picked itself up and slunk off. I never saw the dog again. I hope it was okay.

Max didn't stop there. His next acquisition was a bundle of kittens. They were tiny, real newborns. A few days after Max delivered them to our house, he insisted we go to London to visit his mother. They'd be fine for just the day, he assured me. I was doubtful, but realistically didn't have much of a choice in the matter. As the day wore on while we sat in the restaurant in East Dulwich, I suggested it was time to leave, to check back on the kittens. Max bristled, his ego flaring up. He told me that we weren't leaving yet and that we needed to stay for a few more days. I pleaded with him, but it was no use. He had made up his mind. Eventually, we returned home. The whole journey back I was worried about what we would find when we opened the door. And I was right too. As he turned the key I was hit by a wave of a sweet, sickly smell clawing at my nostrils. There was a black mass of swarming insects in the dining room – a shapeshifting pile of flies and maggots interlaced with pockets of fur and red peeling flesh. Bile rose in my throat, but I swallowed it as I watched Max's expression. There was nothing there. 'Clean this up,' he instructed. So I did.

Later on, he brought home another kitten. This time I was determined to make it work. He still beat the poor creature, splattering its frail body against the floor, the walls, his boots. But I managed to shelter it enough, intercepting it at the right time. This one survived to adulthood, one tiny sip of water, a small scoop of food at a time. His name was Mickey and in the end he lasted years with us.

Two important things happened to me in 1980. The first was that I finally bought a washing machine. The second was that my third child was born, Ivy. By this time Ruby and Jeffery were seven and eight and both in school. My days were filled with boredom and fear – waiting for the children to come home so I could have some sort of purpose, waiting for Max to come home where I'd try to disappear. I was lonely. I needed something to keep my mind busy. I shouldn't have decided the only way to fix this was to have another child, but at the time it seemed the best sort of distraction. Of course, I worried about its safety, knowing that Max would hurt another one of his own. But that didn't stop me.

Surprisingly, though, Max did not hit Ivy. If anything, she softened him. Perhaps it was his age, now twenty-six years old, that had given him the capacity to be more of a father. He still beat me and the other two at his discretion, but Ivy remained bruise-free, her little frame without the dark marks and scrapes that permanently collaged my own.

I was now twenty-five with three children. I didn't know how to be a good mother, but I knew how to not be a bad one. I knew I did everything I could. I loved those children so hard and gave them all that I had. But I was strict too. My own mother was always at the back of my mind, her snide comments and snippy slaps radiating from the locked corners

Me with our three children, bloody tired

inside my head. The only time I slapped my kids was if they'd done something wrong. I remember I caught Jeffery stealing sweets from the corner shop when he was a little boy. Marching him back to the shop to return them was all he needed.

Chapter 7

Australia

First steps to freedom

It was 1971 when Bob the Sailor stole my real father's identity. My mother's brother lived in Australia and she decided it would be a good idea to move there as well. It is 16,488 kilometres from Wellingborough to Brisbane. I was just seventeen when my mother, Carol, Cindy, Michael and Bob the Sailor all left together. Without inviting me. As you can imagine, I was utterly devastated; alone, abandoned and living with Max.

Back then, you could only immigrate if you were a family, with two parents. This is where Bob came back into the picture. He'd been living with Anne, the neighbour's wife, since he and my mother split. But somehow my mother convinced him to move to the other side of the world with her and the kids. I'm not sure if they really were trying to give it another shot or if he was just helping her out so she could start over. But it worked.

Well, officially Frederic Bradbury moved to Australia. Bob had used my father's passport to travel over. I don't know how he managed it, but in those days it was a lot simpler to fake these things. All you needed was a birth certificate, some identification and a marriage certificate. Bob always had a way of getting things he needed. In fact, it all worked out rather well for him. My mother and his rekindled relationship only lasted a few months in Australia, after which he decided to leave and go back to England. Carol told me it was the 'he went out for a pint of milk' scenario. He just didn't come back.

He arrived back at Anne's in England in 1973. It was two years since he'd left, but he'd only managed a few months with my mother. No one was really sure where he went for the other year and half. I do wonder how much of it was all planned. It transpired that he'd gone to the authorities in Australia once he and my mother had split up. He'd told them he travelled in on someone else's passport, convicting himself of fraud. However, this meant he had to be deported. Which essentially got him a free plane ticket home. He was a smart man.

I moved to Australia in May 1983, when I was twenty-eight, with Max and our three kids. My life in Wellingborough was dull, I had no roots there, and I wanted to be near my family, despite my turbulent relationship with them. The idea was first planted a few years earlier. In 1978 my mother married her new partner, Jim Hubbard. They came over to visit and took us on a trip up to Scotland. It was very strange. I hadn't seen her in so long and wasn't used to going on holiday with anyone, never mind her. I had hoped that maybe things would have changed. That the hot sun and lifestyle would have softened her a bit. I was wrong.

I arrived at the airport with Max in the car, ready to pick them up. I spotted my mother and Jim at the arrivals gate and they walked towards us. There was no hug, no kiss, no 'It's nice to see you.' Just hello. The five of us clambered into the car and all drove up to Loch Ness. We marvelled at the landscape, the fells looming over us and the lochs stretching out like shards of glass.

One day, we decided to climb Ben Nevis. I've always been excited by a challenge, and since I've got older, I've discovered a real love of adventure. But, at the time, this was still fairly new to me. We scrambled up the mountain, our breathing laboured and legs aching, but determined to reach the summit. We didn't make it to the top, but it felt wonderful. Afterwards, when we were clambering back down, I felt a dull ache in my bladder and realised I needed the toilet. We were still miles from the car, so I knew I'd have to go alfresco. I called to the others to go on ahead, to carry on. Dropping my pants, I squatted over a small stream. I breathed a sigh of relief, the fresh air on my bottom as I gazed out over the rocks. Abruptly, I heard a crash behind me. Snatching my head around, I saw with horror a goat cantering down towards me, its hooves skidding across the grass, scampering at full speed. I yelped, grabbing my knickers and hastily yanking them up, trying to re-dress myself while avoiding the gushing stream I was straddled across. The goat rushed right past me. I laughed, a wave of glee washing over me, thankful for this avoided disaster. I ran down to catch up with the others, who were plodding along completely oblivious.

We stayed up north for about a week. My mother was not in a happy mood. She sulked, grumbled and shirked, finding things wrong with me and Max and our holiday. Jim tried to keep the peace, boost morale, but it was a slog. I don't know why she acted this way; perhaps her mental health was poor or perhaps it was the only way she knew how to be around me. She didn't ask about how I was or what I was doing in my life. There was no reconciliation for past events or even mention of our lives together. From the outside we seemed like complete strangers.

And, I suppose, on the inside I felt as much towards her as I would to a stranger.

Towards the end of the trip, my mother and Jim told us that they thought we should move out to Australia. I was confused. She'd barely asked about me, barely shown the slightest bit of interest in my life. But she wanted me to go. And that was enough. A small kernel of hope unfurled inside me. My belly began to shift and I knew immediately that this was what I wanted. Even if she wasn't going to be kind to me, I knew that being closer to my sisters and brother would help, would give me some sort of support at least.

'No,' I told her. 'I don't want to go.' Max flashed a look at me. 'Yes,' he corrected me, 'That's a great idea.' He was so predictable. Anything I didn't want to do, he instantly pushed for. He spent so much of our marriage thinking he was in charge, that he was the dominant one. And of course in many ways this was true. But it was at moments like this that I really knew how to get what I needed.

After that everything happened quickly. We sold everything we had. We bought a large, wooden chest and packed it with our kitchen utensils and a few personal belongings. We sent this via boat, chugging across the ocean, mapping out the course for our new life on the other side of the world.

The night before our flight, we stayed at Max's mother's house in Dulwich. It was the 11th of May 1983 and the nights were just beginning to retreat further, the summer evenings yawning with possibility. It felt like the start of something. I barely let myself believe that this was actually happening, that we really were going. Of course, I had Max and the children, but it felt like there was so much potential for change, for the new life that I so desperately wanted. My stomach was a cauldron of nerves, flipping backwards and forwards as I waited for something to go wrong, for someone to tell me we couldn't actually do this. But no one did.

The next morning, Max's brother drove us to the airport. Hope hung in the air, the possibility of safety and freedom imbued in the morning breeze as we made our way into the terminal. I was in a complete daze. Even when we boarded the plane, the children squeezed in, all in a row, sardines in a tin, it didn't feel real. But as the plane took off, our ears popping, bodies pressed back into the seats as it sped through the sky, I finally allowed myself a sigh of relief. I'd done it. Really, truly done it. We were leaving and this could only be a better life.

The kids were restless. Jeffery was twelve, Ruby eleven and Ivy only three years old. Jeffery began to feel sick. One of the air hostesses saw he was feeling unwell and moved him to another seat on his own, just in front where I could still see him. She was kind. Hours later, we eventually landed in Brisbane. We departed the plane, stepping out into the heavy air, the five of us joining the trail of passengers. We went through customs, our passports each stamped dutifully. By this time Jeffery was even more sick, his body leaning on mine, needing to be propped up as we waited in the line. Ruby and Ivy stood upright, their eyes alert, gazing around at this new country they were to make their home in.

As we exited the arrivals lounge, I saw my mother and Jim waiting at the entrance, along with Carol and her husband Randall. I hadn't seen my sister in so long and had never met Rand. My heart swelled in seeing them all there. But of course there was no embrace or emotional reunion. We piled into the car and drove away. I remember the motorway. It was so empty.

All I could focus on was the vast stretch of road, peppered with only a handful of cars. I looked out the window, drinking it all in.

When we arrived at my mother's house, she cooked us sausages. They filled the kitchen with meaty, hot smells, permeating the air and my lungs. Sausages were my favourite food, but these tasted different, probably because they were beef not pork. I wondered if my mother knew this and made them on purpose. The next few days were a blur. Everything was new and different and exciting. Even small things like going to the shops became an adventure. For starters, people often had no idea what I was saying. My sharp cockney accent was unintelligible to the locals and I would have to slowly repeat myself, three or four times over. Going into a bakery one morning, I was truly shocked by the size of the cakes. They were enormous.

My mother and Jim had paid for our airfare. So, I knew that we had to get jobs to start making money to pay them back. Max soon began working fixing cars, but he was not happy about this at all. He didn't like that he owed Jim money and he didn't like that he didn't have the upper hand. Although everything else around us had changed, the dynamic between Max and me had not.

My mother's house was just about big enough for us all to live in. Max and I, with Ivy, slept in the garage, which they'd converted into a bedroom for us. Jeffery shared a room with my brother, Michael, while Ruby shared with my sister, Cindy. This was a comfortable enough set-up. Though one thing that took me a long time to get to grips with was the sleeping schedule. Back home we would stay up late and get up late, but here it was different – everyone slept early and rose early.

So many things were different in Australia, but one thing remained the same. The hot Australian sun had not softened Max, just like it hadn't softened my mother. His rages were just as volatile, if not more so. Now, thousands of miles away from his friends, family and old life, he became vicious, a caged animal unsure of his place in this new world. A particular thing he didn't like was when I learnt to drive. Carol's husband, Rand, was teaching me. I'd putter along in his car, cruising closer and closer to the feeling of freedom. It was this sense of independence, of control over my own time and space that made Max so angry. He could see he was losing his grip over me, sensing that something was slipping from his tight grasp. Of course, this only made him clutch tighter.

One afternoon, we were at a gathering with family and some friends, when Max made a declaration about living in Australia. As time had passed, his feelings of loss and bewilderment had hardened into a strong sense of patriotism. Suddenly England was the best place on earth, the shining beacon of all things good in this foreign land. I felt the opposite. Australia was where I'd felt the safest in my entire life. This was my new home, and no one could make me go back to that old life. Max kept repeating that England is where we were born, that we weren't Australians. He wasn't even born in England himself. But I felt more Australian than I felt British. This sense of community, of freedom and possibility was mine and I was going to fully embrace it. I spoke out against him and said exactly that. His brow thickened, his mouth set into a hard line. We argued right there, in the middle of the party. I was not embarrassed. I was confident in myself, that I had the right to my own opinion, and I wasn't going to stay quiet any longer. He did not like that at all.

Another day, we were at a barbeque with the whole family. It was hot and I was sitting in the yard, Ivy perched on my lap. I was chatting to some other people, but I could see him brooding, a flat look flickering across his face, watching me from across the garden. Suddenly he was standing over me, a beer bottle raised above my head. Spit flecked from his mouth as he threatened me, raising the bottle to hit me over the head. People stopped and stared. I quickly gathered our things and herded the children away, leaving as quickly as I could. We went home, Max, the children and I. I was scared, but it was nothing new. I'd been dealing with this for years. I knew what was in store so wasn't shocked by what had happened. But Carol was.

As soon as we walked through the door, I heard it open behind us. She and Rand stood in the doorway, their faces arranged in anxious expressions. They were stricken by what they had witnessed. They sat down with me, their concerned expressions floating in the air between us. It was then that I realised how worried they were about me. I assured them I was okay, that I was in control. Their exchanged glances did not show they believed me. But for now, there was nothing else I could do.

As the months went by, Max became more restless. His behaviour escalated, his temper flared. Our bedroom in the converted garage had shifted from a sanctuary from my mother into a torture chamber, where Max could get me alone. He'd walk in, grab me, throw me to the floor and twist my arm right up behind my back. A shard of pain would scrape through me, the tendons tightly strained, poised to snap. 'Tell me you love me!' he would command, his sharp breath in my ear. I remained silent. 'I said, tell me you love me!' His voice deepened, grunting through the force. But I wouldn't. I couldn't. It wasn't as if it was a choice really, my tongue just couldn't form the words, even if I had wanted to. He never quite broke my arm, but each time he did it I waited for the clean snap, the crumpled wrench of muscle and bone and skin.

On another occasion, I was walking back to my mother's house from the shops when Max drove the car onto the footpath and tried to run me down. Just in time, I jumped out of the way and ran into the house.

Though I was used to this, my mother was not. For years she'd inflicted pain and misery onto my being and now she watched someone else do her job for her. And she couldn't stand it. We'd been in Australia for a few months when we moved out of her and Jim's house. We didn't go far, just to a small rental apartment down the road, but this only lasted for a couple of months because in November 1983 something unthinkable happened. Something I'd spent years dreaming of, squirrelling away the idea in the back of my mind, always hopeful but never really letting it see the light. One day Max left. He packed his bags and went back to England. But there was one thing I hadn't anticipated, something I'd never considered. He also took Jeffery and Ivy with him.

After Max left, I felt empty. I wandered around my home in a daze, completely numb to the world. My insides twisted, a sharp bile coursing up through my stomach. Vomit splattered over the sink, my loss visceral. I was relieved he was gone, that I didn't have to live in fear of his volatile temper. But I was terrified for the children. How was he going to look after them? How much were they going to suffer? I immediately moved back in with my mother and started trying to work out how to get them back. Max's mother had paid their airfares, so I knew that she wouldn't help me. Instead, I went to a solicitor.

It was a long process. There were so many clauses and holes and hoops to jump through. I thought it might be hard, but I never imagined it would take as long as it did. It was six whole years until Jeffery came back to me and another ten before Ivy arrived.

After years of talking to the solicitor I finally had a court case – in England, March 1986. Miraculously, the Australian Government paid for my flights and all the legal fees. I was full of hope that Jeffery and Ivy would be brought back to me. I stayed at my friends Martin and Diane's house in Wellingborough. I was a clutch of nerves, terrified of the worst. She came with me to the courthouse. It had been so long since I'd seen Jeffery and Ivy, they'd grown so much, and guilt ached in my belly. The court had asked Jeffery who he wanted to live with; he was fifteen by this time and Ivy was six. He'd replied that he wanted to stay with his sister. By this time Ivy had lived with Max for over half of her life, so the court decided she should stay with her father, as should Jeff. I was distraught, my eyes swollen. I couldn't believe it.

The welfare services thought it would be easier to check in on them if they stayed in the UK and assured me that they visited regularly. So I left. My body travelled one way, back across to my new home in Australia, while my heart was dragged the other way, rooted with my two children. I arrived back in Brisbane and went straight to my mother's house, where Ruby and I were still living. I was so grateful I still had one of my daughters.

I'd been on the Housing Commission unit list for years and it was around this time that they finally got back to me. I went around to take a look at the unit. They were lovely spaces, brand new and so much nicer than I was expecting. But the one I'd been allocated wasn't the best. Since Max left, I'd gained so much confidence. So, I thought I'd go and see if I could swap to one of the ones on the main stretch, less enclosed with better views. So I did.

In late 1986 I got a job as a panel beater. It was working in the

Ruby and me in Australia

hot sun, earning $5 an hour to sand down and tape cars. It was exhausting. I'd come home bleeding from the rough sandpaper, my body a weak sack of bones. I absolutely hated it, but I knew working was the only way to get real financial freedom and at this point in time this was all I was qualified for. And money started to pile up. Not quickly, but seeping into my bank account over the months, gradually building up. While I was working, Ruby would come home from school and cook dinner. She's a wonderful cook, even back then when she was only fourteen. I'm so grateful for her during those years.

Chapter 8

Jeffery

A life of torment

I can't remember the first time I read the words 'I'm going to kill my mum' in Jeffery's notebook. I can't even remember how it felt to see this written down, in such brutal honesty. I felt his angst, his wild despair, in the messy scrawl, forcefully scraped into the paper. It was when we still lived together, before he turned twenty-one and moved out. I love my son, but there have been moments when I have been afraid of him. Not just for me, but for what he is capable of doing to himself.

He was around eight years old when I found his pillow stuffed over newborn Ivy's head. We were all still living in Wellingborough, every night waging a battle against his sleepwalking-fuelled misadventures. I'd hear the familiar shuffling, drag myself out of bed to find his room turned inside out, bedclothes strewn across the floor, sheets drooping across the sparse furniture. Moving through my usual routine, I gathered his bedding, reinstating his room to habitable conditions. Almost finished, I glanced over the wooden floorboards, sweeping the room with my eyes, looking for his pillow. Soothing his sleeping mind and bumbling body I coaxed him back into bed. I ducked onto the landing scanning the floor and slipped my head in to look over Ivy. I found his pillow pressed neatly over her head. A bolt of fear kicked into my gut. I whipped it off, bending down to her tiny face. She was breathing, sound asleep.

I walked back into Jeff's room to find him up again, treading the floorboards carefully, his face glazed. Steering him back to bed, I returned his pillow and waited while he settled in. After a few minutes I went back to my own bed. It didn't take long for the shuffling noises to resume. My eyes heavy with exhaustion, I got up again, to find him stumbling away from Ivy's cot, the pillow repositioned over her head. This continued two or three times, and each time I stayed with him longer, trying to lull him into a sense of deep sleep. Each time it felt like he really was asleep, not this transient state of confusion. That morning, when the watery light began to seep through the windows, I knew this couldn't go on. We had to start locking his door. A piece of string looped from his door handle to the hallway banister kept his bedroom shut. And for a while this worked.

Max was so cruel to Jeffery, with meticulous tormenting chipping away at his fragile sense of self. One afternoon, after a horrible berating from his father on his academic failures, Jeff came over to me crying, wet tears slipping down his cheeks. He must have been just twelve years old. He begged me to let him go to boarding school, to let him escape from Max. My heart knotted itself into a tight curl. We were in the midst of planning our exit to Australia, but hadn't told the children yet. 'Don't worry, Jeffery, we'll sort things out,' was all I could manage. His small face crumpled, the angst shining through from his rippling eyes. He was such a strong boy.

A few months later, after we'd moved out to Brisbane, he tried to strangle me. Jeffery, that is, not Max. He crept out in the night from the room he was sharing with my brother, Michael, and edged his way into my and Max's room. I woke to feel his hands grasping around my neck, clutching tightly, his body shaking and hot. I gasped, jolted out of my sleep and struggled to prise his fingers off me. Max also woke but did nothing. I was in shock, deep breaths cutting through my chest, rising raggedly. I knew he had to get help – he was still a child, but the older he got, the worse this could become. But for now, I got him into our bed and held him tightly all night. Years later I spoke to Michael about this and he too mentioned that he was afraid of Jeff although Jeff never hurt him.

Then, of course, I didn't see Jeffery for three years. When Max took him back to England it felt like a part of me had been ripped away. He had some challenges, that was true, but he was still my child, a part of me, and I loved him no less. I'm not sure what happened in his many years with Max, as he doesn't speak much about it, but he did come back with what appeared to be cigarette burns on his left arm.

Jeffery finally came back to Australia on the 27th October 1989, when he was eighteen. Max had said he couldn't cope with him anymore. He was too old for school now, although Ruby was still studying. By this time, I was working as a prison officer and was saving up to buy my own house in Kingston, South Brisbane, though we were still living in public housing for a while. I'd worked so hard these last years and a lot had changed since I'd last seen him. It must have been a shock, returning to Australia after so long away.

No longer in school, he began looking for a job. I was pleased he wanted to work, but after a few months he was still unsuccessful. I knew that he really was trying, but I began to worry. One day, I was in his room looking for something when I found a bong, shoved hastily behind some drawers. Bile rose up in my throat, a dry sticky feeling seeping through my mouth. I turned around, hurrying out of the room and shutting the door.

I hadn't suspected he'd been smoking marijuana at all and I was completely shocked.

Walking into work that day I was devastated. I knew he was mentally unwell, that this was something he'd always struggle with. I also knew that marijuana had a reputation for exacerbating these issues. Had he been getting high while he was living with his father? How long had this been going on? Just knowing that he smoked in a tunnel near my house made me feel nauseous. I didn't want to facilitate this at all. But I knew that if he didn't do it near home, he'd just find somewhere else to do it. All day these thoughts flickered through my mind, a racing stream of micro-realisations and catastrophising.

Over the coming weeks, I couldn't believe I hadn't noticed it before. He slipped between the rooms, out the front door, over to see his friends. He was a ghostly presence, drifting through our lives. Soon, I realised it wasn't just marijuana – he was injecting crack and heroin. He lived with me for three more years, until he was twenty-one. By that time he was really unwell. He would tumble into psychotic episodes, a whole new level of paranoia and hysteria.

He was diagnosed with paranoid schizophrenia in his early twenties in 1999. Once he moved out of my house, he would flit between his friends' houses, sleeping on their sofas, moving on when he needed a change. I worried about him a lot. I'd go looking for him, asking around to see where he was currently living. He always knew where I was, though, even when I'd moved to a new house, he always found me. Of course I'd try to tell him where I was going but he could be difficult to track down. It was at one of these times when I was searching for him that I found him looking bad. A sickly pallor hung over his face, his eyes were dull, and he exuded a jagged aura of impatience. He shifted from one foot to the other, his agitation palpable as we spoke. He told me he'd been prescribed some medication by the doctor but didn't have the money to buy it. My stomach sank, a familiar ache of worry unfurling inside me. I knew I would go and pay for it for him. I knew I couldn't not help him. But I was also unsure if this actually would help him.

When I returned from the pharmacy with the drugs, he thanked me, popping the pills immediately. We said our goodbyes and he left. The next few days, I was a mess, my mind chattering with worry. But unexpectedly he returned home. He was grey, his body weak and it was clear something was very wrong. I put him straight to bed, trying to get him to eat something, but he could barely even keep water down. I was scared for his safety.

His twenties were a tumultuous time for both of us. He would keep a job for a few months but then drop into a psychotic spiral, becoming unable to function as a normal member of society, let alone remember to go to work. It was tough seeing him crumble like this over and over again. He would tell me that people were talking about him behind his back, that they were conspiring against him. It broke my heart every time.

He worked in all sorts of places: in a furniture factory, warehouses, as a forklift driver, that sort of thing. I once found him asleep outside the warehouse he was working in at the time. He'd spend his days at work, then head over to the cinema and then go back to work to sleep outside. There was a little spot tucked away round the back behind a shed where he would stash a sleeping bag. He'd wake up in the morning under the open skies and wait for his boss to arrive and make him a cup of tea. I thought it was odd at the time that his boss didn't mind him doing this, but now it makes more sense. Jeff didn't want to be constrained inside a house; he felt safer outside, in the open, where he felt he was in control. At this point I just wanted him to feel safe, whatever that meant for him.

The only time I was ever truly afraid of Jeffery was in 2001 when I was living in a rented place out in Moorooka. I'd left my job at the prison and was then working in a doctor's surgery as a receptionist. I'd got the job through my own doctor – he'd told me there was a position going so I thought, why not. Anyway, one morning Jeffery walked through the doors. I could tell within an instant that he was not okay. His eyes were wild and there was a look of detached bewilderment burning across his scrunched-up face. 'I need to see a doctor,' he said, his voice rolling. 'No problem,' I replied. He sat down in the waiting area, muttering to himself. I saw the other ladies glance at one another, before one of them leant over to me and said, 'He's talking to himself.' 'Oh,' I said as I threw him a glance, confirming their diagnosis.

The doctor came quickly after that, ushering him into a consulting room. I watched the door patiently. Jeff was almost thirty years old and this was not the first time I'd seen him in this state. A few minutes later, the doctor called me in. The doctor got straight to the point. He turned to Jeffery and asked, 'Can you please repeat your name for me?' Jeffery stared back, unblinking. 'Jesus,' he replied coolly. The doctor tried again. 'No, what's your real name?' And again, Jeff said plainly, 'Jesus.'

By this point the doctor was ready to call the ambulance. He could see that Jeff was in the midst of a psychotic breakdown and needed to be somewhere safe under medical supervision immediately. Straight away I took him to the PA Hospital where I coerced him inside and tried to calm him, to talk him around. Sometimes this worked; a lot of the time it didn't. He was becoming more agitated, more frantic by the second. He stared at me, his mouth dropping open. 'Mum! You're so famous!' Calmly, I asked him why. 'Because you're Mother Mary,' he proudly declared. At this point I could see it was only going to escalate. It was difficult to keep him in the room. He kept trying to leave but I really didn't want him outside. I was fearful he wouldn't come back.

Eventually I had to let him go out for a smoke. I watched, my eyes trained for the slightest movement, any sign that he might make a run for it. But suddenly his chaotic energy faltered, his body relaxing. He looked up slowly, raising one hand to the sky. 'You want me to heal people now? No! You want me to destroy myself?' A shiver ran through me. I'd seen him hurt himself so many times, seen him try to hurt me. But this possession, this full detachment from reality was frightening, silently creeping through my bones, sending prickles of dread over my skin. I knew then that he had no control over his actions from here.

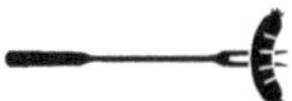

Every time Jeffery would have a psychotic episode, he'd eventually wind up in hospital. It was where he needed to be, to be properly looked after. They'd sedate him, he'd feel better and then they'd release him. He'd take their medication for a while, feeling much better. Then, when the drugs were doing their job, helping him function and be himself, he'd stop taking them. He felt he didn't need them anymore, that he was better. And, of course, the whole spiral would start again.

It hurt so much to see him going through this pattern; it was as predictable as the sunset. In 2003, I got a phone call at work from the hospital. 'We've got your son here, something really bad has happened and I don't know if we're going to be able to save him this time.' The words fell like hammers on my ears. Stunned, I stood up. A woman from work drove me home and I called Ruby and Ivy. My husband, Robert, arrived quickly and shuttled us to the hospital. We burst through the doors, catching Jeffery before he was taken into surgery.

It was horrific. He'd cut his eyeball with a knife, nicked it right in the centre. He'd also cut his throat. A rough, jagged slash across his neck, his windpipe spilling out, loose and flapping under his face. His torso was covered in wounds: eight stab marks, each one carved out in a passionate thrust. There was a lot of blood. His face was dazed, his eyes barely seeing, his slack mouth hanging loose. I clutched him, whispering, 'Oh, Jeff, I really thought you were going to stay with me this time.' A mangled noise dribbled out of his mouth, before he managed 'Oh no, Mum!' That was it. Then he was wheeled away to surgery.

Everyone went home except me, Ruby and her husband, John. I spoke to the nurse, who said it was one of Jeff's neighbours who had called the ambulance. Jeffery was living over in Woodridge, in a small rental unit. He was under the Woodridge Mental Health clinic and every week a nurse was meant to go in and check on him. But one of his neighbours had seen a pool of blood outside his door and had immediately called for help. It turned out he had cut himself the night before, then paced around the building before lying down on the couch in the dining room. It's a wonder he lived.

There'd been another incident a little while before. I'd been in to check on him and the unit was a mess, rubbish littering the floor, unwashed dishes lying around the room. This was a bad sign. Jeffery was a compulsively cleaner, like me, so I knew things were going to take a turn for the worse when his hygiene started to waver. I came back a couple of days later. The neighbour had called me again, and said he was worried about Jeff. As I opened the door, I saw the noose swinging from the ceiling. It was empty. My stomach dropped, but I didn't falter. 'Jeffery? Are you here?' I called out, scanning the room. My eyes fell upon a pool of blood in the bathroom, splashes of it spattered across the sink and the floor. He wasn't here. I carefully untied the noose, mopped up the blood and started to clean up the room. This wasn't the first time I'd walked in to find this sort of scene.

Clozapine. That's the medication Jeffery was on. It's the only one that works for him, makes him feel okay, able to cope with the world. But the problems begin when he stops taking it. The side effects are grim; they grind him down and when he thinks he might be all right this time, he'll take the risk and try to come off them. It was on one of those days, when he'd decided to stop taking his medication, that he marched down to the police station, butter knife clasped in his hands, his body tingling with manic energy. Slipping through the doors he marched right up to the front desk. He grabbed the knife, thrusting it towards the first officer he saw, thrashing it around, trying to catch something with the blade. He had a ripe smattering of bruises around his neck and blood blooming across his shirt. Once he was restrained and safely sedated in the hospital, he told the doctors he just wanted to be dead, go to another planet, and wanted one of the police officers to kill him. Suicide by cop he called it.

Trying to kill a police officer was the best thing Jeffery could have done. He was charged and put under forensic order. That meant he was an involuntary patient, unable to discharge himself. After the windpipe incident, he was moved to the mental institution at Wacol, Wolston Park. Now it's called the Wacol Centre for Mental Health. He was detained there and stayed for thirteen years. Once they thought he was safe enough to be let out on his own, there were little units scattered around the centre where the more stable patients lived, able to come and go and have more freedom, while still being supported.

I would go and visit him all the time. I'd take him out for a cup of tea, a walk, just something for him to look forward to, to have some change in his life. Thirteen years is a long time to live somewhere and by the end I knew the staff really well. We'd always have a chat and they were so brilliant to Jeffery. Looking back, this place really saved him. Every Sunday, the centre would organise a trip outside for the patients, taking them somewhere else for a bit of normalcy. But then, of course the government cut their funding, so I took him out on Sundays instead. I was outraged when the funding was cut, it was a lifeline to so many of the people living there.

Around this time, I was put in contact with a journalist, who was looking into the cuts. We arranged an interview and I spoke to him about how important it was for Jeffery and the many other people who relied on Wolston Park. Once his article was released, it began to gain traction. Miraculously, it reached the right people and the funding ended up being reinstated. I was overcome with joy. Walking into the centre once news had broken was emotional. So many people came to thank me. I was really proud of that.

But while this was going on, Jeffery had slipped through the cracks again. I have such respect for the people who work in these institutions but there were holes in the care system. On one visit, I was walking with Jeff, when I noticed blood stains leaking through his t-shirt. He'd been cutting himself again and they hadn't noticed. I'd felt so safe knowing he was here, that he was being looked after, but realising they were not as thorough as I thought was difficult. Shortly after this he tried to slit his throat. Again.

When someone cuts their own throat, that triggers alarm bells. Except that here it was a constant cacophony of alarm bells, drowning each other in a mess of noise. This is how they missed that Jeffery was cutting himself. He was slitting bits of his torso, gouging himself. He's been so unwell for so long now, nothing shocked me anymore. But this was difficult to see. Once the staff finally realised this, he was locked away in a secure part of the centre. Somewhere with closer monitoring, for people who were a true danger to themselves. I don't know much about what it was like in there, but that was where he lived for two years.

Going in to visit, it felt like a prison. You had to get through multiple gates, being screened and checked just to get in. He was in the highest tier of restriction, just below the criminally insane. It was a shock when he was released. In fact, it wasn't just him, it was all of them. The centre had decided to let them back into society. They gave him a Housing Commission unit in Cleveland, shipped him in and left him to get on with it.

Cleveland was okay. I looked after his money for him, did the food shop, and bulk bought all the essentials. When I dropped by one afternoon, the unit looked tidy and he seemed calm. Relaxed, I scanned the room, checking that everything seemed in order before settling on a lovely tea towel covering a plate. I flipped the corner, peering underneath at a piece of quality raw steak, placed neatly in the centre. 'What's this for, Jeff?' I asked. 'Oh, that's just for God to come down and eat,' he replied nonchalantly. Right. I didn't argue with him, just made sure to check in each day. Sometimes there was steak, sometimes it was a glass of milk. But always in the same place, God's corner.

One night in August 2019, I got a call. Jeffery was on the other end, his breathing ragged, his voice strung with tension. 'Mum, I've gone too far this time.' 'What is it?' I asked. He'd sliced off a piece of his thigh. The upper inside part. He'd run out of steak and God was angry, hungry, so he'd had to make do with what he could offer. And that, of course, was himself. 'Go to the hospital,' I replied calmly. I'd heard it all before. Nothing could faze me at this point. I knew panicking wouldn't help anyone. I was blasé. It was just so normal now.

He took himself down to the hospital in his car where they stitched him up. He stayed a little while but was soon back in his apartment. It was a routine he knew well. The next time I saw him he was covered in bruises and scrapes. He told me there'd been a fight between some of his neighbours and that he'd got involved and tried to intervene. I gazed at his battered face. He was always trying to help, always getting caught up in the middle of something. He has such a kind heart, but sometimes doesn't realise when to stop. I'd do his food shop but then he'd give half of it away to the skinny lady across the street. He was trying to be kind, but it hurt to see him taking care of others but not himself.

I knew that he would flicker between sobriety and using drugs. By this point it didn't faze me, I just wanted him to be safe. A lot of his neighbours were heavy users. They would steal from him: food, money, anything they thought could be valuable. Jeffery had been learning how to drive, and once his neighbours realised he had a car, they would sweet-talk him into letting them use it. I helped to buy him that car, and it hurt to see it being used to run drugs around. Because of that, I regularly clamped it until he was well enough to drive again. It didn't end well. I bought him two or three cars over the years and eventually had to stop. Helping him didn't seem to be actually helping him anymore. I couldn't carry on supporting him and eventually Ivy had to take him in to live with her. I just couldn't.

He stayed with her for a little while. But it couldn't last forever – they both needed their own space. So I found him an apartment just up the road. This was not a good time. I spent a lot of time there, calling up the police and ambulances. He was in a really bad way. His neighbours began moving out. They were scared of him. Day and night, he would be talking to himself, shouting and screaming in the street. Coming on and off his medication drove him mad, flipping him about from one delusional state to another. It was getting dangerous for all of us. At that time, he was forty-nine years old.

Next, he moved into Greenslopes, into an assisted housing unit for mentally ill people. Nurses would come in and check on him, see if he was all right. But there were also a lot of recently released mentally ill criminals living there. I didn't want him to get involved with this again, so he now lives near me. It's a one-room apartment, funded by the NDIS. Every morning and evening, support staff go in to give him his medication. When he thinks he's going to hurt himself, to relapse, he'll tell them or tell me and then go off to the hospital. It works better this way.

He's now fifty-one years old. I rang him last Sunday, spoke to him on the phone. His voice was raspy, cracked and dry. I asked him if he was sick, but he told me he was fine. I was confused, but we just carried on with our conversation. Then on Monday he popped over to my house for a cup of tea. He does this a lot now; we see each other all the time. His voice was still gone, and I asked him if he was sure he was okay. 'It's from all the screaming, Mum,' he said. Ah. It was the voices, screaming inside his own head, the ones that never leave him alone, no matter how medicated he is. Schizophrenia is a terrifying illness. I don't know how he's made it this far if I'm honest. 'I just went into the bathroom and had to scream back at them,' he told me blankly. 'I just can't take it anymore.'

Of course, I feel guilty about Jeff's illness. It breaks my heart to see him suffering like this and there's always the question creeping in the back of my mind whether I could have done more to help him. I'm not sure what but surely something. Last week he wanted to talk about his funeral. At first, I assumed he was planning mine. But he wanted to know if I thought he should be cremated or buried. That was a hard conversation. It's difficult to know that he's tried to end his life so many times, but even more so to think of him actually succeeding. You never expect to outlive your children. But he's just had enough.

Ruby will give him a call every now and then, especially if I can't get through to him. Or if he doesn't want to talk to me, she'll see if he wants to chat with her. I always worry when I can't reach him. When he's psychotic, I'm the one he wants to attack. He'll storm round to my house, bubbling with frenzied energy, throwing accusations at me. The paranoia seeps in and he thinks I've turned him over to the authorities, sold his secrets and his soul. I always try to keep a physical barrier between us during these incidents. The kitchen bench, a table. He really has no control when the psychosis sets in. Once he's come down, climbed out of the psychotic state, he is so gentle. The staff at the hospitals have only good things to say about him: his softly spoken manner, his generous heart.

After one incident recently, when he burst in demanding money, he got quite scary. Yelling at me, pointing, jumping up and pouring his tea on the carpet, at the same time staring arrogantly into my face. He knew it would upset me, but I appeared to stay calm. It sounds like a small thing, but he knows how much of a clean freak I am. He would never do that if he was in a balanced state of mind. Anyway, he became more threatening, more violent. I kept calm, trying to talk him down, console him and eventually he stormed off. At that time, I really felt in danger.

I've told the doctors before that it was frightening when he was like this, that he is an actual risk to my safety. But they don't do anything about it. Just tell me to alert the authorities when I fear for my safety. A load of bullshit. So this time I recorded it. Set up my phone and taped the whole thing. I brought it to the doctors, showed them the recording. Immediately they sent someone out to look for him, saw that he was a danger to society. Sometimes he just needs to be locked away. They found him that night pacing the streets, a knife tightly clenched in his hand.

Chapter 9

Prison

A career behind bars

I cheated on the entrance exam to get into the prison service. There were around eight people, all seated along this large wooden table, and I cheated off every single one of them. I didn't want to; I could have answered any of the questions myself if someone had read them out and helped me write the answers. But that wasn't an option. So I glanced over at their papers, their curved, flowing writing gliding across the sheets in front of them.

I've spent my whole life struggling with writing, so this was nothing new. You learn to pick up tricks, little shortcuts to help out in these kinds of situations. A quick glance, a drop of the pencil to lean over. I'm ashamed that this is what it had to come to, but it was the only way a lot of the time. I put my head right down, scanning across everyone's paper, their answers laid out in full view for my perusal.

It was 1988 when I applied to work in the prison service. I was thirty-two. In the end I worked there for six years. I'd been working as a panel beater but wanted more. I wanted financial freedom. I knew I needed to get a more skilled job, something that would always be in demand. My brother-in-law, Rand, worked in the prisons. He earned decent money and said it was a steady job. I thought, well, why couldn't I do that too? So one morning when I was down at the dole office I realised I was ready. Ruby was getting older, so our allowance was decreasing, but she was still in school. As I was filling out the details on the form, I knew it was littered with mistakes, but I just didn't know where or what. As I handed it back to the administrator, he raised his eyebrows, clearly expecting very little from me. The familiar pang of shame kicked my abdomen, but this time it was accompanied by rage, rage at his assumptions about me. My resolve thickened. I would show him that I was capable of getting any job I wanted.

After the entrance exam, walking to the train station I was feeling deflated. I'd given it my best shot, copied so meticulously, even the notes and workings out. But I knew that they would see through my efforts and realise I was a fraud. However, one night when I was making dinner, the phone rang. I picked up and to my surprise it was the prison service offices. 'We'd like to invite you for an interview,' they explained. I was overjoyed. I knew once I was in the room with them, I'd be able to show them that I was more than capable. Hope flooded through my body, settling into a smile in the corners of my mouth. I carried on making dinner.

The interview was a breeze. The questions were self-explanatory, and I had an answer for everything. I remember one of them asked, 'If you have a TV to give to one of the inmates, how do you pick which one will get it?' and I replied loftily, 'The one who is the best behaved, of course.' I felt like this was something I really had a chance at. The thought of violence didn't faze me either. After all, I'd spent my entire life surrounded by violent, cruel people. If anything, this felt safer – at least these ones were behind bars.

But in the end, I didn't get in. There was a three-month course starting in April and I didn't make the cut. So many people had applied, they said they just didn't have the resources at that moment. Of course, I was disappointed. I really thought this was going to work out for me; I'd dared to let myself be hopeful that this could be the start of a new part of my life. But not this time. For weeks I sat with this sadness and carried on going about my life, cooking, cleaning, looking after Ruby. Until one evening the phone rang again. A woman who was meant to be on the course had just broken her leg. Was I still interested? Could I come in? 'Yes, of course,' I said. And that was that.

When I showed up for the course, I was fizzing with anticipation. I knew there would be more writing, but I also knew I'd be able to worm my way around that. In the classroom a few days later, one of the men sitting next to me leant over and asked how I'd managed to get a place here. He could see my writing was a mess, jumbles and squiggles tunnelling across the paper. But aside from that, I knew I was good. We had gun training, restraint sessions, all the physical stuff. I was able to wriggle out of a headlock, fire a gun and avoid capture just as well as anyone else in there.

But the writing continued to be a problem. Even when I cheated, my eyes flickering over other people's handbooks, allowing me to write down the correct answers, it was obvious that this was what I was doing. It had been almost twenty years since I was in school, in that old brick building in south London. But I knew that if I really wanted this job to work out, I'd have to go back.

I was living in Kingston with Ruby, and just around the corner a night school had opened. I'd kept my eye on it for weeks now, stealing sidelong glances at the information about the Reading and Writing Help for Adults Course that they ran. The first day I walked into the building, my knees were quivering. A thick lump had risen in my throat and my breath was short. I sat down in a creaky chair, pulling it right up to the table and waiting silently for the class to begin. It felt strange being back in a classroom after all these years. I was deeply uncomfortable, tension knitting between my shoulder blades as every mocking remark from my childhood schooling prickled at my eyes. But I was steely in my resolve that I would do this. I clenched my jaw and listened.

In all honesty, the night school course didn't solve my problems. It helped a little, that's certain, but I didn't emerge a linguistic butterfly, dancing through a plane of prose and poetry. I learnt about the I-O-U-S in words and this really did change my life; I had no idea I'd been spelling so many words so incorrectly before. But in the end, I just hunkered down and got through it. It certainly gave me a little more confidence and I was proud of myself for doing it.

There were two teachers leading the class and at the end of the course they went to speak to the prison service course leaders. They told them I had a problem with writing and that I would need extra support. I was both horrified and grateful for this. It meant I didn't have to pretend, to keep it so secret, but the shame of people knowing burned from inside. Before I left, one of them pulled me aside and said that if I ever needed any help to come and let her know. I was touched by this, but never did. The Superintendent, a lady called Stack, told me when I started at the prison that I was to go to her if I had any problems and she would help me.

One of the lead officers on the prison service course was named Sheila. She hadn't been on the panel when I was interviewed. On one of the days, she turned around to me and spoke directly, telling me that if she had been on the panel, I would never have been accepted into the course. I was taken aback, even though I knew I was different from the other students – for starters they were mostly men and the other woman was a lot bigger than me, a bit tougher. I was tiny, still am, but I knew how to behave in these situations, knew how to use my size to my advantage.

It was on the prison course, at Wacol College, that I met Robert. At the time I thought nothing of it, but six years later he would become my husband. There were thirteen people on the course in total, but only one other woman. But I was strong-minded and I held my ground, and after the three months were done, I was transferred straight into the prison.

My first day was terrifying. I arrived at Boggo Road prison, my uniform crisp, my nerves soft. A woman named Lynn met me at reception. She was to be my mentor, the person who would teach me the ropes. I managed a thin grimace, my anxiety evident. I followed her down the maze of corridors, walking through the building, to the cells, the common areas, the canteen. As we passed by, the prisoners leered, whistling catcalls our way. It was a female prison, but the attention still threw me, made me hyper-alert, feeling tightly scrutinised. Lynn cocked her head, staring at me. 'They don't always do this, you know,' she said.

I felt self-conscious. I'd turned up in my full uniform and cap but soon realised no one else was wearing their hat. My cheeks burned red and I quickly took it off. It's funny, looking back I remember how petrified I was, but it wasn't of the prisoners. It was of the other guards; the idea that I might have to answer the phone or take notes or file some documents. The fear of administrative errors cut far deeper than that of physical violence.

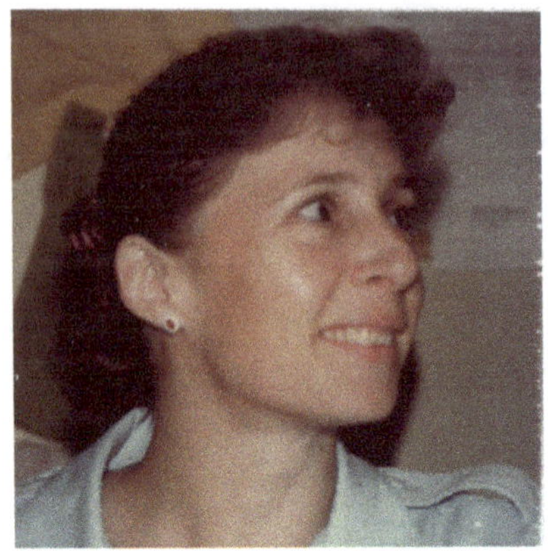

Me working in reception at Boggo Road

Because I was so concerned about being caught out, being uncovered as a fraudulent imposter, it meant my memory skills were slick. As I couldn't make complex physical notes of when prisoners were moving about, visiting the medical centre or going to take a phone call, I had to memorise each person's whereabouts. While this did not please a lot of the other guards, my memory really improved. It helped me feel strong even though it was due to my biggest weakness.

I worked on the prison gates as well. There were two opposite each other, one at the front and another to the prison itself. I worked on them both, shuttling people, cars and information between each gate. It was exhausting; you had to keep tabs on everyone coming in and out. It was so busy that I was kept running most of the time, but I enjoyed the interaction with people and organising the records.

I felt powerful working in the prison. I must have had an underlying desire to be in control, be in charge when I applied, because after a while working there, I realised why I loved it. Not in a manic, power-crazed manner, but the fact that I didn't feel like the underdog, like I was out of control with things just happening to me. This time I was on the other side, the person making the decisions. The very things that had brought me such sadness and suffering throughout my life – violence, fighting, abuse – were now some of my strongest assets. I knew how these people thought, why they might act a certain way, and I wasn't afraid of a scrap. In fact, I loved wading into a fight, trying to pull the women apart, diffuse the chaos before any real injuries ensued.

That's not to say I always got it right though. While I was still new, I'd only been working there a few weeks, one of the prisoners tricked me. She was a kleptomaniac. It was a burning hot day, the heat hanging heavy in the building, thick and sweaty. As you can imagine, it was not a pleasant environment to be in at these temperatures. So one of the prisoners came to me to ask if she could return to her cell to get some deodorant. I couldn't see the harm in that, so I took her down, following her lead. We entered the room and she grabbed the deodorant and a couple of other bits and pieces before returning to the rec room. That was all and I just carried on with my day. The next morning, I was pulled aside by another guard. She told me that this woman had not taken me to her cell, but someone else's, stealing some of her possessions.

I was horrified that I'd been so naive; embarrassment crept up my neck, spreading a redness across my face. I expected her to report it so I'd be reprimanded, but she didn't. It was common for newbies to get manipulated by the inmates, as they pushed you to figure out what they could get away with until you had become hardened. It was the best lesson I could have had. As a result, I became vigilant, watchful. It turned out that before she was incarcerated, the prisoner in question had in fact stolen a baby. That made me feel slightly better. She knew what she was doing.

I knew that when I first started, people would underestimate me; I've been underestimated my entire life. But it's never stopped me proving anyone wrong. One of my tasks in the first few weeks was to take the muster before mealtimes. This was like a register, where the officer calls out each prisoner's name and they answer, stepping forwards as they speak. The room was quiet, and the prisoners stood in line, waiting for me to start. But as I began, they weren't complying, were not stepping forward, just answering lazily. They took one look at me, a slight, timid-looking woman and thought I would be a pushover, an easy target. But they were wrong. Of course, at the start I was nervous, my voice small and soft. But as my confidence grew, so did my presentation. When they didn't step forwards in time or muttered under their breath, I would call them out and make them all start again, because they were anxious to eat, and this kept them from their food. I could see they were taken aback. They didn't think I would be a tough one. But I knew it was the only way to retain respect.

As the weeks went by and I settled in, my authority grew. Even though my surname was Rahman, I was sometimes affectionately referred to as Rahmy by some staff. When the prisoners went off, swearing and shouting at me, I would remain calm. Calm but strict. I'd stare them dead in the eyes, my gaze penetrating their vulgar insults. 'Am I swearing at you?' I'd ask. Of course, sometimes they would retaliate, spitting and snarling back at me. But as time went on this became less frequent. They understood I was no-nonsense and I wasn't going to rise to the bait, but more importantly that I was fair. I treated them as the people they were, regardless of what they had done.

But sometimes the steely glances and sharp words aren't enough. When there was a physical fight, I'd have to intervene. The first time I did this I could tell everyone was surprised, not just the inmates but the other officers as well. Some of the staff would just disappear, hide away from the conflict and wait to pick up the pieces afterwards. That was never going to be me.

There were two prisoners scrapping, viciously pounding each other, grabbing and thwacking and punching. I was standing close and saw the raw energy leap from woman to woman. I ran over, my shoes squeaking on the hard floor and jumped straight onto the nearest woman's back. Hooking my left arm around her neck, I used my right hand to snatch at her nose, dragging it backwards towards my body. Clearly struck by this unexpected intervention, the woman complied, more out of confusion than submission, but it worked. Seeing what I was trying to do, to drag this woman away, one of my fellow officers slipped behind me, opening the door to her cell. I steered us both in, my fingers still wedged firmly under her nose.

This became my routine for when I needed to break up a fight. I'd calmly tell them that if they did not comply I'd just dig my fingers in further. You'd be surprised how much pain you can cause this way. It was unexpectedly remarkable. But I never wanted it to come to violence. When a situation needed intervening, I was the first one in. It was almost like a rush, the adrenaline gushing through my veins, sloshing in my ears. However, I was never an instigator.

There were two types of disciplinary charges in the prison: a major and a minor. Naturally, both required a written report, so I tried my best to avoid these altogether, though this wasn't always possible. I found it was best to start with negotiating, trying to persuade prisoners to do it your way. I recall sitting on a step while working in the maximum security section one day, trying to convince this woman to come and help the others with some work. It wasn't really optional; they each had to pick a job and do it, in exchange for a few dollars. It seemed like an all right deal, if you ask me. But she wasn't cooperating, just sitting there refusing to move. So I sat and talked, cajoling her into making a choice. I told her that even though the best jobs had been taken, they weren't really the easiest, they just looked it. 'Oh yeah?' she replied, her face a granite sheet. I dug harder, 'Of course, the real easy ones are still left, they just sound like work so no one picks them.' An eyebrow arched, her gaze still intact. I was lying, of course, but it did the trick. She clambered up, standing tall as she sloped off towards the others. Pride tickled at my shoulders, resting in the space under my heart.

Moments like this weren't necessarily common, but they weren't few and far between either. I overheard a couple of prisoners talking in the yard once. They seemed to be deliberating over something and I saw one of them shrug and gesture over to me. The words 'Go talk to her, she'll listen' drifted over the general murmurs. I think that was why I was good at my job, because I listened and wanted to help some of them, like a prisoner who couldn't read or write. I made sure she got into a literacy class without having to wait for the system to get around to her.

Being so trusted by the women was flattering but it also meant I had to deal with some difficult conversations. A couple of years into working there, a few of the inmates had come to me about another woman. They said she was refusing to shower, and the smell was becoming unbearable. This sort of conversation with anyone would be sensitive, so I was anxious about approaching her. But, true to form, I was calm and strong-willed, explaining that washing was not an option and she needed to just do it. Understandably, she got upset. I didn't enjoy doing that at all.

Being liked by the prisoners was one thing but it took me a while to find the same respect and friendly nature in the other staff. If I had to pinpoint when I began growing closer with the other officers, I would say it wasn't until the next wave of trainees came in. It must have been about a year. I would see the other officers all in the maximum security office together. There was a real pecking order. I would sit in the rec room with the prisoners, just watching and waiting. I knew I'd end up in their cliques soon enough, but I wanted to get a grip of the hierarchy first, to observe them. I've always been like that: I like to get a bearing of the situation before I choose who to befriend. I'd learnt the hard way that you have to be careful who you can trust.

Once the new batch of trainees joined the prison, I felt my rank move up. I suddenly held more weight with my colleagues, as well as in the eyes of the new recruits. One day, a tiny slip of a woman sat next to me in the rec room. 'Do they pick on you more because you're small?' she asked meekly, gesturing to the inmates. 'No,' I replied loftily, because it was true – they didn't bother me any more than some of the guards.

One of my favourite jobs was working in reception. The police would glide through the front doors, bringing with them the new prisoners, fresh in from the free world. They were often crying, distraught and panicked. My role was to sort out their paperwork, and get them organised and ready to enter the jail, settling them into their new purgatory life. It sounds depressing but I wanted to point them in the right direction.

The women had to stand in front of my desk while the charges were read out to them by either me or the senior officer. Reading was fine, I could happily do that without worry. The senior officers would stand too, rigid and watching, everyone alert for any sudden movements or flashes of anger. But mostly the new prisoners were still in shock. Then everyone else would disappear and it was just me, the new prisoner and one other prisoner to hand out clothing and toiletries. Then they would go to have a shower and get into their clean clothes, before being taken down to maximum security.

Generally, the younger they were, the more upset they would get. Tears would trickle down their colourless cheeks, their bodies rigid with fear. Or sometimes they would sob, huge, racking shudders electrifying their bodies. Others were silent, a dull fog surrounding them as they moved noiselessly through each instruction. I would explain that they were heading to maximum security. That under no circumstances should they sit at the front. Sometimes I was afraid for them. There were some very dangerous women down there.

Then I'd lead them down the corridors to the unit. I'd always give them to another prisoner, pull them aside and ask them to look out for her. A usual suspect was Valmae Beck. She was a child killer, convicted of murder, but a safe pair of hands to entrust the new inmates to. Surprisingly, she always looked after them.

Drugs were a common problem; so many women were using in the prison. I handled a few drug busts over the years and what struck me the most is how much the women changed when they were high. Some were slack and non-responsive, other times they had superhuman strength, pulsating with frantic energy. These were the times that made me careful, when fighting became dangerous.

The prison had become overcrowded – so many inmates and not enough staff to work with them. We were stretched enough as it was, and the few weeks prior had felt strained. I was doing my usual rounds of the building, walking through the garden, peering into the rooms in demountables that were installed for the overcrowding. I glanced through a window and saw two prisoners sitting next to each other, a spoon gripped between their fingers and a lighter held up underneath. Instantly I turned on my heel and ran to get back-up. I pushed open the senior officer's door, my breathing sharp and fast, and she came rushing with me to the scene.

We arrived panting, shoving open the door to find them already high, the slither of smoke sucking into their lungs. Eyeing us, they both stood up. We moved quickly, jumping atop each woman, restraining their arms and heads. Drugs were a serious offence. They both kicked back, their strong bodies convulsing and thrashing, trying to shake us off and break free. We struggled to keep them constrained in the long corridor. I could see the rage, the wild desperation flashing across their faces as the drugs flooded through their veins. I heard the running footsteps of other officers coming to help us. I just held on, digging my fingers tight into the woman's arms, pinning her to me. The officers arrived, prised her off me and took her away. I stood there, my body tingling, arms fizzing. It was an exhausting rush every time.

Drugs weren't even the biggest problem. There were a lot of mental health scares, suicide attempts. As you know, I have a lot of experience with people who have mental health episodes. I sometimes wonder if I attract them, if they know something I don't. One particularly nasty one occurred one day when I was once again just doing the rounds, walking back and forth between the wide corridors of the jail. The prisoners were all locked in their cells. The usual clattering of metal against the bars suddenly intensified, and shouting began. I ran towards the commotion, immediately seeing a dark figure swinging from the ceiling. A thrashing body sharply convulsed, legs twitching, torso shaking as the noose tightened around her neck.

I grabbed my keys and fumbled with the lock, before shoving

open the door to the cell. Stepping under the woman, I grabbed her legs, pushing her up, holding her in place. She continued to thrash but let me help her. I knew she didn't really want to die. Another officer carefully untied the noose, letting her slip down crumpling to the floor. Sweat trickled down my forehead and my shoulders ached under the weight of supporting her, of trying to keep her alive.

Suicide attempts were common, but not for the reasons you'd expect. It wasn't until I worked in the prisons that I realised how backwards the system really is. You see, while a prisoner is in jail, they can't earn any money, except for a couple of dollars doing odd jobs here and there. However, if they are committed to the mental health ward at Wolston Park, then they are eligible for the dole. As a result of this, many inmates stage a suicide attempt in order to be transferred to the psychiatric hospital. I remember the first time I realised this, I was in total shock that this was how it worked, and it was eventually stopped.

The prisoner that I stopped hanging herself was a common offender. It wasn't her first time trying this. She was desperate to go back to Wolston Park. After I'd saved her this time, we ended up in a scuffle. It was outside the laundry room and she hit me. A strong thud, right across the back. Pain shot through my body, but I didn't have time to process it as I knew she'd be ready to hit me again soon. I had the keys in my hand – they were chunky metal ones, huge and cartoonish. I whacked her, the keys gripped firmly in my palms, and the metal dug into the skin.

Tussling, I saw a shadowy shape to my left and out of the corner of my vision Storm Brooke appeared. Debra's murderer. A stab of fear jolted through my body. This was not good. Bracing myself for an assault from both sides, to my surprise she was not here to join in. Well, she was, but she was actually here to help me. Storm pulled off the other prisoner, gave me time to get my bearings and grab her again, this time putting her into a hold. Storm watched as I thrust my right hand over the woman's stomach and my left wrapped around her neck. I plunged my fingers in, locking them on as tight as I could manage. By this time, I could hear other officers running towards me and I knew I just had to hold on for a couple more seconds. Her writhing body ripped at me, as she used all her strength to try to tip me off, but I held steadfast. 'Get her off of me!' she shrieked.

The officers had to prise my fingers off her. One by one, they peeled them back, restraining and slowly releasing her one digit at a time. I was frozen in place, breathing heavily as they led her away.

Storm Brooke was a murderer. She had come to Boggo Road from down south and she was tough. She'd been brought up to be a fighter, running drugs for her father since she was a child. She stood no chance really. She'd been known to carry a gun down her trousers. And bloody hell she could fight. Working in the prison showed me what real criminal life is like. Max's petty crime was pale in comparison, childish games from a long-ago distant life.

It was dinnertime and the inmates were being ferried over to the canteen, filing down the long corridors. Storm joined the snake of prisoners, leaving her cell and walking towards the kitchen. I saw her stumble, collapse to the floor. A guard sidled up to her, calm and collected. We assumed she was weakened or just vying for attention. But as the officer got closer, her movements sharpened and she quickly dragged Storm into an upright position, shouting for help. Storm was covered in blood, unconscious.

I ran to her cell. It was important to find out what she'd done, what she'd used to hurt herself. We could see it was a self-inflicted wound, but we were worried what else we might find. I unlocked the heavy, metal barred door of her room. It was bare, normal inside. Except for the water jug sitting in the middle of the floor. It was full to the brim of blood. Deep crimson, sticky liquid, congealing in the vessel, thick and opaque in the glaring overhead lights. Bile rose up in my mouth, the metallic taste of my own reaction combining with the iron scent of the contents in front of me. I stepped back, locking the cell and returning to the other guards.

She was taken away in an ambulance, the jug of blood alongside her. We were used to violence, to self-harm and suicide. But less so this eerie, premeditated behaviour. I went with her in the ambulance, sitting with her, holding her hand. She'd asked me to do this, clutching at my arm like a frightened child. Though I complied, I had no sympathy for her at all, I couldn't have cared if she lived or died. I'd seen her kill Debra and knew what she was capable of. Knew that she felt no remorse.

Once we arrived at the hospital, they stitched her up. I sat next to her watching it happen, the needle tugging on her skin, gliding through her doughy flesh. After the repairs, a doctor pulled me aside. He glanced at Storm and then back at me, giving me a puzzled stare as he explained the situation. The jug hadn't been just blood. It was half water. Ah. So it was another cry for attention. Logically I knew that she must be desperate if she was willing to do this just to shock us, to have something to do, but I had no sympathy for her at all. I sometimes wonder if she did it just for a change of scene, an excuse to leave the prison. It sounds awful but it was the kind of thing the prisoners would admit to. Jail certainly isn't a place for rehabilitation.

After she'd murdered Debra, back in January 1990, Storm and the other attacker, Amarlie, had been taken to solitary confinement. The rooms were bare, with nothing they could use to hurt themselves with. My shift had ended but because of the chaos that was still around the place, the senior officers asked me to stay on a bit later. I was exhausted but agreed. I could always use the extra money and it wasn't like I was going to really say no. I escorted Storm and Amarlie to their new cells in the male division medical centre and stood guard outside. After a few minutes Storm came to the doors. She asked me for a pen. My brain was foggy with the day's vicious attacks, and I didn't think at all before handing it over. In retrospect, it was a serious mistake.

Minutes later, I heard a noise from inside the cell. A guttural, animal sound. The other officer and I quickly unlocked the door, barging inside to find blood gushing from her arms. She'd snapped the pen, using the plastic to gouge into her flesh. We dragged her to reception and called the ambulance. In a daze, I sat on a bench waiting for the emergency services to arrive, swinging my legs. My mind was blank; I had nothing left to give. I felt empty inside.

Once the paramedics arrived, one of the officers explained that I had given her the pen and that it was my fault. I knew that this was true, so I didn't argue. I felt so numb, I just didn't care anymore. But worse was to come: I was required to stay back and write a report, creating another stress trigger. I did get help from a fellow officer with the report but I was a mess.

Finally, around ten o'clock in the evening, I went home. I must have looked haggard, as a couple of the officers offered for me to come and stay at theirs so I wasn't alone. But I just wanted to go home, to be with my children. I started work again the next day, another shift because officers had resigned and we had to fill the gaps.

I've been told that I have no filter when I'm speaking. To an extent I agree, but in 1991 when I was asked to join the negotiating course run by the Queensland police I was perplexed. Did they really want someone who couldn't censor what she said? Another woman, who was far more senior than me, was also interested. However, they picked me, and it turned out I was bloody good at it.

The training was back at Wacol College and again it was mostly men on the course. We'd have scenario workshops to prepare us for the real situation. The first time, the teachers got us up one by one, to engage with an actor pretending to be a criminal. All of us failed. It turned out he was deaf. It was things like this, that you wouldn't even think of considering, that you had to learn to recognise. They'd link it to real situations that had happened in Brisbane, to help us equate our job to the real world. It was mainly just keeping calm and talking, two things I can be incredibly persuasive with.

For the final part of the course they brought in a police van full of all the equipment they'd use. We were siphoned off to another room with a huge whiteboard standing in the middle. I was terrified they were going to try and make me write on this. It's almost laughable, there I was practising to negotiate with terrorists and all I was afraid of was writing. Anyway, luckily, I was chosen to be in charge of the communication, just talking to them. They had specially trained actors, briefed to make it as difficult as possible. A lot of what I learnt boiled down to blaming my boss. If we couldn't meet their demands, tell them it was out of our control and so on. The whole thing was surprisingly simple. But I suppose if you're the right sort of person it will be.

They made it realistic, though, screaming abuse, recounting the gruesome things they would do to the hostages if we didn't meet their demands, trying to make you squirm. They'd talk about vulgar, horrific, sexual things, try to throw you off, but working in a prison already, this sort of talk wasn't new to me. I found that if you matched their tone, flipped their questions back at them, it often worked well. I'd just chat as if they were friends.

This final test carried on for the whole day and night. They had to make it as realistic as possible, so by the end you're exhausted. It's all about learning how to keep calm and make good decisions under pressure. The questions were intensely personal, and they even asked me what my preferred sex position was. Without blinking an eye, I told them it was on top. Sadly, after two hip replacements, my body wouldn't do that for me these days. The course helped me a lot in my own life as well, which was rather unexpected. Fortunately, I never had to put any of this into practice. It was one thing in a no pressure, sterile environment, but I didn't want to have to test my abilities in the field. I know I could have done it, but I also know I'm glad I didn't have to prove it.

I left Boggo Road in 1993. I suppose you could say I had a breakdown. Officially I went on stress leave, but I knew as soon as I walked out of the gates that I wouldn't go back. It had been one of the best jobs I'd ever had, but it had also broken me. By this point I had become a walking skeleton.

It all started when they brought in male officers. As it was a women's prison, it made sense to only have female guards, and everything changed when the men came in. They were confused about how to handle the inmates. When breaking up a prison scrap, they wouldn't know how to restrain them respectfully, whereas we all knew you just had to do what you could. After a while, they became less worried and settled into the routine. One of the new officers was Robert, from my training course. Since the course we'd not spoken, but now that I saw him every day we began to talk more. In time we started dating and eventually married long after I'd left the prison.

Meeting Robert was wonderful, and he made my life so much fuller in so many ways. But, it made it far more difficult to separate work and home. This was part of the reason that my mask began to slip. I used to arrive at work, game face on, and disassociate from my real life. This made it easier to separate out the trauma that I was witnessing daily from my own feelings. It meant I could leave at the end of the day and not carry home the emotional weight of the job. But once I met Robert, my guard was let down. I opened up in my personal life, became more vulnerable with him and then couldn't switch this back off at work. And it was exhausting. Absorbing the pain, suffering and injustice of everything I was exposed to chipped away at me, sucking the joy from my soul.

One incident that really struck me happened after this. It was the beginning of my decline, and I remember thinking at the time that I needed to keep an eye on this, that I couldn't let myself become affected by the incidents or it would break me. Well, that didn't quite turn out how I'd hoped. There was a new inmate in the prison who was a transgender woman. I was working at the gate and she had come up to ask me a question. Then, from behind her a male officer appeared, placing his hands over her eyes and back. She stiffened. He removed his hands and walked away. I was livid. I spoke to him later on, reminding him that our job here was to protect the inmates from themselves and each other, not to manhandle them. I had begun to attach my own emotions to the goings on in the prison. But to be good at this job you have to be logical, meticulous and pragmatic. This is where it all started to go wrong.

I began to have panic attacks. I'd just be standing at the gate, conducting a walk around, and my head would start pounding. My breath would quicken, my vision would blur, and a rising sense of impending doom would creep up my throat. It felt like I was going to die. The prison decided to change our working patterns, so we'd do three months in one section and then rotate to another three months later. This meant working with the same prisoners every single day. There was no respite, no break. If you were placed with some challenging inmates, you were stuck with them. I was moved to the medium security unit.

Valmae Beck, the child murderer, was in my unit. So was Lisa Ptaschinski, one of the vampire killers. Alongside her girlfriend and two others, she'd been involved in murdering and attempting to drink the blood of their victims. Unsurprisingly, she had a lot of difficulty with her mental health and every day would come to me with a new issue. It was draining. She sucked the life out of me. While spending time with the same inmates allowed you to understand how best to deal with them, it also taught them how best to manipulate you. This was a terrible mistake. I began to feel like a shell of myself. I'd wake in the night, my heart racing, sweat pooling on my back. I knew then that this couldn't go on much longer.

Afterwards I had PTSD. I would drive around the streets, fully on autopilot, not realising that I'd driven past my house already. By this point I was living with Robert and over the next few months I didn't really leave the house without him or Ruby. It was a dark time. Robert really did save me, but over the next few years he would also break me.

Chapter 10

Robert

Real love

Before I met Robert, I hadn't dated in ten years. I suppose you could say that my relationship with Max had put me off men for good. I needed a long time to recover from that, to be able to even consider letting anyone in again. I did try a dating agency briefly, but it's safe to say that it wasn't very successful. I met three men from the agency. The first was a tax agent, and he wanted to just marry me straight away. Big red flag! The second was a fisherman, who basically wanted a housewife to cook his dinner for him on his boat. No thanks! And finally, there was a man who was very short and I had nightmares about dating very small people for a long time.

After that, I didn't even think about men for a long time. I threw myself into my work, trying to save up for a house and gain some financial security. I was living in public housing with Jeffery and Ruby. Every week when the bills would come in, I'd run straight down to the post office to pay them straight away. Having autonomy over my finances was life-changing. I didn't have to worry about having enough to eat or steal from the electricity box. It was a whole different world. I felt strong and independent.

It was 1990 when I finally saved up enough money to put down a deposit on my first house. It was new, $55,000, in Velorum Drive, Kingston. I'd gone to the Westpac Bank to ask for a loan. Now that I had a stable income from working in the prison, I thought they would grant me one easily. But on sitting down at the shiny plastic desk with the adviser, I was told this wouldn't be the case. Without a partner to split the cost of the mortgage, they weren't prepared to lend me the money. I was livid. I felt discriminated against. I left the bank simmering with rage. The next day I went back and closed my account with them. I didn't want to support such a sexist policy.

But I still needed some help to raise the extra ten thousand dollars I needed. So I went to my sister, Carol. She and Rand lent me the money and I was able to put down the deposit on the tiny house in Kingston. I was so proud of myself. All those double shifts at the prison, all those years putting five-dollar notes into jars from the panel beater's. Growing up with nothing means it's a lot easier to live on practically nothing. By now the poverty of Wellingborough and London felt a long way away, a fading dream.

It took me nine months to pay Carol back for the loan and soon after this Ruby left school, so she began paying rent to live with me. It felt so safe to finally have my own space, somewhere that no one could take away from me.

As I'd mentioned, everything changed when the men came into the jail. The institution had the idea that they would integrate the male and female prison staff. I suppose they thought it might be helpful to have influence in both jails. But it changed the dynamics of the place completely. On one hand, it felt less pressured, almost like it balanced out the intense female atmosphere. On the other hand, some of the men acted a bit tough. At that time, I saw Robert as a charmer.

Surprisingly, he was not the first person to compete for my attention although I'd never felt so sought after in my life. There were men asking me out from all over the jail; at one point there were four men trying to attract my attention. I wasn't used to this at all, and though I was of course flattered, it wasn't what I was looking for. One man was very odd in his pursuits. He would ask all sorts of unexpected questions: 'Do you like waterbeds? Is eating meat wrong?' Safe to say, he did not warrant a date. Another man would just sidle up to me at work and say, 'So, when are you going out with me?' with a leering smile plastered across his face. He asked me on duty, while we were doing walks of the corridors, in the office. He was very persistent, but again it was a hard no. One man would even send me flowers. That was rather lovely.

But it was Robert that I decided to take a chance on. We'd chat and laugh together at work; in fact, it was the prisoners that picked up on our flirtation before I really realised it was happening. One day he asked me if I liked museums. My heart squeezed a little in my chest and I replied, 'Yes please.' I loved museums. I was excited and it was a lovely trip. Afterwards Robert asked me if I wanted to go and get something to eat. By this time, I was happy to agree, sure that he would know somewhere. But the nice little restaurant I had pictured turned out to be McDonald's. I wasn't so impressed now.

The thing was, though, I liked Robert. He felt safe and kind, the sort of man who would look after me, wouldn't hurt me. Though I needed to be sure about that last point. Years of battery from Max had made me wary. It had taken so long to claw my way out of that prison, so there was no way I would go back.

I decided that I should start a fight with Robert early on, see how he reacted, and make sure there wasn't an angry monster hidden inside. So I tried to start an argument, causing a scene over some small inconvenience. But he was just confused. I'd raise my voice and he'd just stop and listen, try to talk to me about it. I was shocked. Well, I suppose I didn't have to worry about his temper then.

After we'd been to McDonald's, he turned to look at me and asked, 'Do you want to come back to my place?' 'Certainly not,' I replied. 'I won't try anything, I just like spending time with you,' he said. Well, I had enjoyed our date and wanted to spend more time with him too. So I went. We talked for hours and when we finally went to bed, I remember lying there in the dark, in his one-bedroom apartment, thinking about how much my life had changed. Then, out of nowhere I heard this loud 'Parp!' He'd farted right next to me. I thought, how uncouth! Somehow this didn't put me off at all. From then on, we were dating. I did get him back some years later when I was lying naked on the bed talking on the phone when he came into the room, saw my exposed crotch, said, 'Mmm ...' and put his head between my legs. At that moment, I farted right up his nose. I was crying with uncontrollable laughter as he reeled back in horror, calling me a dirty bitch, and ran out of the room. I call that karma. He would try and get me every time I went to the loo in the night. Climbing back into bed half-asleep, I'd lay my head on the pillow and then have to sit up coughing and spluttering. He'd fart into my pillow and then pretend to be fast asleep. In fact, he was choking with laughter. After that, I got into the habit of coming back from the loo, picking up my pillow and smashing it repeatedly over his head. It didn't take long for him to learn the error of his ways.

Robert made me feel safe. He was tall, very strong, with thick tattoos snaking across his limbs. In all the years we were together I never felt threatened by him or anyone else for that matter. He was the protective force that I so needed. He was a loud man, always making jokes and ribbing with people. I suppose you could say he was boisterous, very fun to be around. This was one of the reasons I liked him.

The morning after our first date, I woke up in his tiny apartment. He'd separated from his ex-wife so was living in this rental unit for the time being. I remember feeling so glad that I had my own place. We went to work like nothing was different and carried on meeting up, going out together. As we began seeing more of each other and spending more time in each other's company, I began to notice some discrepancies in his behaviour. Waking up one morning in his bed, I was alone. I heard the clink of glass in the kitchen and poked my head around the corner to see where he'd got to. The morning light shone through the illuminated bottle of spirits that was being shaken upside down above his open mouth, his head tipped back. It was 7 am.

I knew this wasn't a good sign, but I thought it wasn't that big of an issue. He was having a bad day and needed a little help sometimes. This should have been a bigger warning. I also began to notice that he never had any money. Our dates would either be free things, or I'd end up paying. I wasn't prepared to spend my life at McDonald's, that was for sure. Eventually he admitted he was spending it all on renting the flat and paying child maintenance to his ex-wife. Of course, this made sense. But the empty liquor bottles still piled up.

I began to get frustrated by his prioritisation of partying over me. He would go off to Sydney with his friends, go clubbing all night and then come back in a right state. Sometimes I'd see him at work, sunglasses pushed deep down over his eyes, his movements slow, like his head was made of stone. This was when I knew he'd been out all night and was suffering from a heavy hangover. I'm not a big drinker, enjoying only a glass of wine from time to time, but it's never been a big part of my life. When I was in England, I was too poor to drink, so I never really got the taste for it. However, I could see that for Robert it could be a problem, it just took me a long time to realise how bad.

Mostly I was just upset that he was prepared to spend money on drinking rather than on me. It hurt when he would come around and say he couldn't afford to take me out for dinner but could easily piss away the evening in a bar. After a few months of dating, I said this to his face. He didn't really take on board how serious I was about it. I think he chose to not listen properly. So I decided enough was enough. I wasn't going to stand for this. I said, 'Right, well, we're splitting up then.'

I could tell he was shocked. But he didn't argue, just agreed. In reality, though, he didn't stop anything. He carried on pursuing me at work, asking me to go out with him again, or if I wanted to see him later on. Looking back, I can see that he needed to be babied, that he wanted someone to look after him. It's funny because I told him from the start that I wasn't going to be a housewife, that he could go and cook his own damn dinner. But this never swayed him and he still wanted to be with me. Of course, having someone wholly devoted to being with you is a wonderful feeling. After a while of separation, we eventually started dating again. This time it felt different. We both understood each other more, knew where we stood.

But it turned out there was still a lot I didn't know about Robert. For starters, it was the gambling. Financial awareness and money had become of huge value to me. Growing up without much at all had instilled this. I didn't need lots of it but having control over my financial situation was imperative. Somehow I let Robert get mixed up in all that. Since putting the deposit down on my house, I had continued squirrelling money away, saving it for the future. But when he started talking about wanting to move from his one-bedroom rental to a little apartment closer to work I couldn't help listening. He didn't quite have enough for the bond money. He was still paying child support for his kids and all his earnings went on his rent. And the drink, but I was still oblivious to this reality. So I gave him the money.

It's so hard when someone you love asks for something that you know you can give them, that you know will make them happy. From the outside I could see that maybe giving him money wasn't the smartest decision, but from my heart it felt right. Being with Robert had opened me up, made me vulnerable again. I'd let my guard down with him, the first person in a very long time, and I didn't want to give that up. That feeling of being looked out for, of having your worries halved becomes addictive. It was so much easier having someone you could depend on than having to do everything alone.

He took the money and moved into a two-bedroom unit in Marooka. I got to see Robert's children more. Melinda was twelve and Kevin was fourteen and I liked them very much. He had two older kids as well, who were twenty-one and twenty-two, but they lived away from home so I didn't see them very often. I was living in my house in Kingston with Ruby and, fleetingly, Jeffery whenever he wasn't couch surfing with his friends or on the streets. The children all got on fairly well together and it was lovely having such a large extended family around. I'd always wanted to be part of a big loving family, and finally I had it.

Eventually it made sense for me to move in with Robert. Robert had paid me back the money that I'd given him for the bond. So I packed up my things and moved into his place. Ruby and her boyfriend stayed at my house in Kingston. They were paying rent and it was nice for them to have their own space as well. A little while later I went overseas to a wedding in Hong Kong with Carol, my mother and Jim. I'd not travelled much at all and it was wonderful seeing another part of the world. I came back tingling, excitement bubbling through my veins. I wanted more of this, more chances to see the world, to go to new places and do such different things.

I spoke to Robert, babbling about how much I'd loved it, how the experience had opened my eyes and that this was what I wanted to save my money for. He nodded. I explained that I needed to save up as much as possible and that this meant I'd have to move back into my own house. You see, I'd been paying rent at Robert's and it just made no financial sense. He was sad but understood. He could see this was important to me. He asked if he could live with me instead. I agreed but told him he'd also have to pay rent. 'That's absolutely fine,' he replied.

Ruby, on the other hand, was less pleased. She'd gone from having the whole house to herself and her boyfriend to suddenly having her mother and stepfather squeezed back in. She was protective of me, as she'd seen how I'd let men run all over me in the past and was wary of anyone else coming in. She watched over me like a hawk, always keeping a sharp eye on Robert, on how he was treating me. It was cosy, but I loved everyone living there together in the house that I bought.

Shortly after came one of the worst decisions I could have made in our relationship: a joint bank account. At the time it seemed like a natural thing to do. We both had steady jobs with similar incomes, Robert was paying me rent and our outgoings weren't too high at all. After all, I was still an excellent saver, meticulously pocketing every spare penny into my savings for our trip abroad. One morning, I checked the account to see how much we'd managed to save. Four thousand dollars was missing.

My stomach lurched. That was a lot of money. I knew that I hadn't touched it, so with a sinking certainty I knew that Robert had.

Shouting was never effective with Robert. I guess that was one of the reasons I liked him – we didn't solve our problems with aggression, just with talking. So I confronted him, asked him where it had gone and what he'd spent it on. 'I needed it,' he replied, his voice quiet, embarrassed. I was puzzled. 'What could you possibly have needed four thousand dollars for?' I hadn't noticed any big purchases and didn't think he was in any debt. There was a pause, the air hanging heavy over us. I saw him take a deep breath, his eyes meeting mine. 'Gambling!' It felt like a kick in my abdomen. Thousands of my hard-earned dollars being thrown away on a frivolous whim, for the cravings of a dopamine hit. Anger surged through me, mixing with horror. I had no idea he was a gambler.

Realising that he kept secrets from me was tough. Especially ones that were going to affect me too. It had taken a long time for me to save that money – depriving myself of little treats, always buying the cheapest brands in the shops, being so careful about each cent. I was raging but I was mainly disappointed. I felt betrayed. I said this to Robert, watching his face twist in angst. Good, I was glad he felt guilty. He'd not just stolen from me financially but he'd also stolen the future I'd been planning. I could see he felt awful – but it didn't stop him doing it again.

This was around the time when I had to leave my job at Boggo Road. I was on stress leave and was really mentally unwell. By the end I could barely recognise my own house in the neighbourhood, never mind thinking about planning a trip overseas. I always thought it was work that was too stressful, the prisoners' emotional baggage spilling over into my own life. But I now realise that I had pressure coming at me from my home life too. The struggle of dealing with distrust and lying from Robert combined with the chaotic world of Jeffery and his illness meant I was being assaulted from all angles. Ivy was also with me; she'd arrived back to live with me in 1993. I had no respite, no space that was calm and safe and my own.

Being with Robert had broken down the barriers between my professional and personal life and I just couldn't handle it all anymore. So I left work and for the coming months morphed into a shell of the woman I'd been previously. I needed help with the most basic tasks and barely left the house without Robert by my side. Although he was a root cause in part of the problem, he was also my saviour. I know I could have got through it with Ruby helping me, but he really was there for me too.

I was bad, really bad. Walking from the lounge to the bathroom I would get confused, just standing in the hallway. Robert would come in and ask if I was okay, what I was trying to do. I'd stare blankly back at him, having no idea myself. It was a frightening time. The pounding of my heart thudding in my chest, constant palpitations thrumming through my body, accompanied every waking breath. I'd have panic attacks. I couldn't really go outside. I knew my family was worried about me, but I didn't have the capacity to think about them, I couldn't even think about myself.

One day, we got a phone call. It was a lawyer, contacting me about my stress leave from work. At this point I was on workers compensation, still getting paid from the prison. But the lawyers explained that given the trauma I experienced at work, I had a case to sue the government. Even in my frazzled state I was shocked. That was just my job, to protect the inmates, it was the kind of violence you have to be prepared for if you sign up to work in a jail. But the lawyers were adamant that I had grounds for a higher payout, that the government owed me for the situation I'd been put through with the murder.

They had found me through the doctors. As part of the deal with workers compensation, I had to see a psychologist and a psychiatrist. So I managed to drag myself out to the appointments, Robert helping me to leave the house and arrive at the right place at the right time. The psychologist talked about the murder. How I'd felt, how it was affecting me. The psychiatrist went deep into my history, my family, my previous marriage, everything. He took a lot of notes but just said, 'Hey, make sure you keep seeing your psychologist, okay?'

It was the psychiatrist who tipped off the lawyers. He'd been at a party in the city and one of his friends was a lawyer. They'd decided I had a case, so he got in contact. They eventually convinced me to have a meeting with them, so Robert and I drove into the city. We sat down and I told them everything: how I'd cheated on the entrance exam, how I could barely even spell. At the end of the discussion one of the lawyers turned to me and told me they would take the case and would do it pro bono for a while. I had no idea what this meant so I just nodded and smiled meekly.

In the end the whole process took nineteen months. It was hours of negotiation, of talking in cramped offices. It didn't ever go to court, just back and forth, from solicitor to solicitor. In the end I got a payout. It was $165,000. I was shocked.

By this point Robert and I were engaged. In fact, we'd got engaged in September 1992 before I went on stress leave when I was still at the jail. This amount of money was life-changing. I sold my house out in Kingston and we decided to build one ourselves.

During the nineteen months of negotiations I'd slowly come back to life. I was able to complete small tasks around the house, drive down the street, and remember where I'd put my shoes. I felt my body waking up from the crushing, ghostly world I'd been trapped in.

We managed to take a trip, to finally travel like I'd wanted. We went to Bali, took a cruise and saw the sights. It was wonderful. But I knew that I really wanted to build a house. I wanted to do it right, so we got a mortgage and we built the most beautiful home.

We built it in Munruben Forest. It was rural, a one-acre plot in the forest. Robert and I lived there with Ivy and Robert's sister, Sheryl. I really liked Sheryl – she was a kind, fun woman and for a while she was my best friend, but she wasn't half gullible. She lived with us for almost seven years in total. I've mentioned that Robert was a prankster and he enjoyed joking around and playing tricks on people. He soon learnt that I didn't enjoy being the focus of his little set-ups so unfortunately Sheryl was often the target.

One night, Robert and I were asleep in bed when there was a deafening crash and our bedroom door burst open. Sheryl was standing wide-eyed and panicked in the doorway, scratching frantically at her head. 'There's a spider in my ear!' she hollered. In a sleepy daze I just stared at her as she swatted and tugged at her ear. But Robert, always ready for an opportunity to poke fun, quickly replied in earnest, 'Quick, go outside and put a hose in your ear!' Poor Sheryl sprinted from the room, clattering down the hall into the garden. I heard the faint whoosh of the hose pipe turning on and her quiet yelps as the freezing water drenched her head. Robert chuckled to himself beside me, but I felt bad. She rushed back inside, dripping water behind her, proclaiming, 'I found the spider but it's missing one leg so it must be still in my ear.' Before we could say anything, she was on the phone to the hospital. Of course, they told her to stay calm and that it would fall out of its own accord. She really did lack common sense sometimes, but I loved her for it even more.

I can't be too quick to judge. I have had many naive moments myself. Sheryl and I were in the garden one afternoon, pottering about in the sun. Robert walked up to us dangling a huge brown wispy thing from a stick. 'What snake is this from?' he asked us. He dropped it on the ground and we all peered in closer. It was husky and dry, with scaly, flecked patterns over one side. I was curious and Sheryl scooped it into a bag to take into work to show her colleagues.

The next day she returned from work, red-faced, annoyed and embarrassed. She'd brought it in and unwrapped it in front of everyone, to have them all burst out laughing at her. It turned out that it was the bamboo wrapping of a garden flame torch. As she told me this story, I heard a gasping bout of laughter erupt from behind me. Robert stood clutching his ribs, beside himself with glee. I was rather embarrassed too, thankful that I hadn't humiliated myself in front of anyone. He could be thoughtless sometimes like that.

One of the most hilarious discussions I had with Sheryl was regarding chicken teeth. She was just convinced that chickens had teeth. I was perplexed, but she was so adamant that it was true that I almost began to believe her. But then she started to explain how we actually breathe out of our belly buttons and I knew that I couldn't listen to a word she said. She was a very smart woman; her downfall was that she just believed a lot of what she was told without questioning it.

Robert and I had some great times in Munruben. We had a spa in the ensuite and one evening we were having a few drinks in the tub. He got up for a smoke and I just lay back relaxing, enjoying the feeling of the bubbles against my skin. A few minutes later he came back. The plug had been pulled out, but I was lying there in the bubbling water. I was very drunk by this point and I climbed out yelping and ran around the house completely naked, screaming in delight.

In the mid-nineties I was able to fully work again. I got a job at the doctor's surgery, as a receptionist. It was when Jeffery was particularly bad. Robert had also left the prison service by then. After I'd left, he'd been moved to a different department, where they kept the child molesters. The things they would say would leave him pale and when he came home each night I could see he wasn't himself. He'd seen what had happened to me, how work had shattered my very essence, draining my spirit. He was not prepared to go through that himself, so he got out while he still could. The problem was, he didn't get another job for a while. He couldn't find anything stable and was between work a fair bit.

I wasn't paid as well at the surgery and we began to struggle with our mortgage. I was supporting us both: bills, food, everything. He was also a smoker and began complaining that he couldn't even afford cigarettes. This angered me, as I was giving him an allowance, going out to work every day and still handling all the expenses. 'Right, you do it then!' I said, exasperated. That didn't last long, and sheepishly he handed that responsibility back to me soon after, with a new appreciation for my abilities to balance our spending on such a limited budget.

He soon stopped talking about money. I assumed it was because after his short stint in control of our finances he realised it was more difficult than he thought. But then one day I was looking at our mortgage repayments. They were just getting beyond me. It was at this moment that I realised we were in trouble. That Robert, in fact, was not a safe man. That I should have jumped ship a long time ago, that first morning that I saw him emptying the liquor bottle into his mouth before work. He had taken out a second mortgage on the house. He had forged my signature, gone behind my back and lied to me. I crumpled. Anguish rippled through me, my legs became weak and I sat down. This was the moment I should have left him for good. But I didn't.

Sheryl was a gambler too. She lost her car. With the second mortgage and supporting Robert, I just couldn't keep the house. Putting it up for sale was one of the worst things I'd had to do since Max left. What hurt the most was that the reasons I had to give it up were not of my doing. Robert was bleeding me dry, even with the huge payout from the prisons. I was devastated and angry.

I couldn't bear the idea of moving somewhere new, but there wasn't another choice. So I sent out Robert and Sheryl to find our house. They found one in Sunnybank Hills, which we bought and moved into. I absolutely hated it there. Sheryl moved in with us, but Ivy didn't – she went to live with her boyfriend, Murray. She was almost nineteen by this point. But this house didn't last very long at all. Robert was unemployed, and trying to sustain two adults on a receptionist's salary was near impossible. So we had to sell up again. Next, we moved over to Moorooka, this time just renting, my ambitions of being a homeowner dissolving before my eyes.

Working at the surgery one afternoon, the telephone went off. It didn't feel like it at the time but picking up this call would start another chain of events that would change my life yet again.

I picked it up. It was Robert. After a minute or so of chit-chat he announced, 'I'm going to start a welfare course.' I was shocked at this snap decision, the authority in his voice. 'Okay, sign me up too,' I replied instantly. He was a smart man, but I was also a smart woman. I knew I couldn't work as a receptionist forever, I needed something more. Something more for my finances but also something more for my soul.

I did weekend work at the surgery while we studied full-time to become welfare officers. It was a bit of a whirlwind really, but I absolutely loved it. I loved going into the school every day. My writing skills still hadn't come on in the past years – my breakdown had slowed any progress I could have made – but that wasn't an issue. On my first day, I marched straight up to the teachers and explained my situation. They listened carefully, reassured me that they would be able to work around this and that there wouldn't be an issue. It felt right to be back in the classroom. This was different to the night school I'd attended before, even different to the prison officer training program. I felt like I was meant to be here, like I belonged.

Robert sat all my tests for me. He wrote out my assignments, took all of our notes. I've never been great at retaining large amounts of information for exams – it's just not one of my strong points. But as soon as I'm out on the job, it all floods back and I know exactly what I'm doing. I'm so grateful for Robert's tireless help with the course. He was a gem.

Around the same time I became ill. It was 2001 and after I'd been to the doctor's for some discomfort they told me I needed bladder and bowel surgery. They also suggested I get a hysterectomy as well, so I agreed. Money was tight – I didn't have a job as we were both on jobseekers' allowances while we completed our training course and now the surgery put a lot on my plate. But I knew I would come out the other side strong and ready to carry on. While I was in hospital, Robert would come in to visit, but he'd always ask for money. I had to hide it around the apartment: behind the fridge, under a chair, inside a shoe. Each time he asked, I'd direct him to another hiding place. In retrospect I can see how unhealthy this was, what a child he was, but at the time it had just become my normality.

He did try to leave me once, when we were living back in Kingston, still working at the prison. One morning he'd just turned around and announced he was going. His son had called him up on the phone. I stared at Robert, my face blank. 'Okay then,' I said calmly. If that was what he wanted. He sighed and began packing his things. Minutes later the phone rang again. It was his ex-wife. I could hear her tinny voice whistling down the phone line. I watched Robert's face contort, his eyes roll and his shoulders sag. Eventually he put the receiver back down. 'Actually, I think I'll stay. I can't go back to that.' And that was it, he stayed. He realised I wasn't going to cause drama, wasn't going to scream and shout and wail. But he just wanted to be looked after, for someone to mother him. So for a while this is what I continued to do.

The next few weeks after my operations were difficult. My bladder was barely functioning, and I just felt so weak. The flat we were living in was small and had cramped stairs up to the first floor. I was in so much pain that I could barely climb them, so I always needed help getting up there. To add to this, Ruby and her husband, John, were staying with us while they built their own house. Ruby and Robert looked after me so well though. My bowels weren't working for a while, so I had to be assisted with going to the toilet. It was when they both started arguing over who was going to have to do my enema that I knew things needed to change, that I needed my independence back. Slowly I began to get better and had another operation to put me back in control of my own body.

Once I had recovered, I wanted to get straight back into work. I completed the welfare course, undertaking a placement with Autism Queensland at Wellington Point. I was working with three autistic ladies and I absolutely loved it. Once that placement came to an end, I was certain this was something I wanted to do with my life. I walked straight into a job with Autism Queensland, where Robert soon began working as well.

Money was still tight, so we decided to leave our rental place in Moorooka and move in with Sheryl and her daughter. Sheryl had lived with us for years and I'd helped her out so many times, so it felt fitting for it to be the other way around this time. However, the situation wasn't quite ideal. Robert and I lived in their basement, sleeping on a mattress propped up on bricks. Drifting to sleep each night, my eyes heavy, I would ponder on how much my life had changed in the last couple of years. Building the house out in Munruben seemed like an eternity ago, so far detached from our current situation. Sleep permeated my consciousness, and I would settle down dreaming of how things were going to change again, how I would turn this into something brilliant.

We moved out of Sheryl's in 2002. Through scrimping and saving, hiding away every single cent of my wages, I'd managed to save enough money for another house deposit. I'd sat Robert down, told him that I needed this, needed to get back on the property ladder, regain my independence. Earnestly, he agreed, and said that we would do this together. I bought a house in Acacia Ridge. It wasn't much, but it was a start, the beginning of my road back to redemption. It was truly lovely, and big enough for Sheryl to move in with us. I loved living with her, and she paid us rent as well, which certainly helped keep the place up. But she then tried to get a loan to buy a yacht. She needed $22,000, but couldn't raise it. So I gave her the money.

Robert emptied our account again. We couldn't keep up the mortgage payments, so had to sell again. I was too numb to be devastated. I wasn't even surprised any more, just exhausted by this cyclical pattern. Once I realised we would have to sell the house, I decided it was time for something new. I needed a change to break this cycle. So we also bought a yacht in Manly, Queensland.

It was Sheryl's idea. She had stopped gambling but was frittering whatever money she earned away with no control. It was so bad that she was blacklisted everywhere, across the whole of Brisbane. Rental agents wouldn't lease anything to her, and between her and Robert, I was afraid their incapacity would tarnish my own name.

Robert's continuous draining of money from our account had sucked us both dry. We just had enough after the sale to scrape the money together for our own yacht. At this point, I was still working at Wellington Point, with the three autistic women. Desperate to save our finances, I was taking as many shifts as I could manage. But each time I started to build up a little nest, Robert would siphon it off. His gambling had become out of control. Four or five thousand dollars would disappear at a time.

I don't know why I couldn't stop him, couldn't stop letting him take the money. But it was just so difficult to say no. After a while I was sick of living like this. I loved being on the ocean but needed four walls around me, needed some more space. So I told Robert and Sheryl I was going to move back into a townhouse. They were welcome to join me, but I had made up my mind that I needed this and neither of them was going to stop me. I settled on a place just up the road, still in Manly. Robert and Sheryl both came with me. We sold the yacht and packed up again.

This time I made certain things would be different. I stopped using our joint account and put all the rental agreements in my name alone. This changed everything. Suddenly I felt like I was back in control of my life. I could see the path towards a future of security and an end to this stressful circus of cohabitation.

It was in this home in May 2007 that Robert started a business that offered accommodation and community support for people with intellectual, physical or psychiatric disability with his business partner Kerry. I worked in the background, helping with the details and planning. On paper it was split fifty–fifty between Robert and Kerry, which suited me just fine.

Building up our own company together was exciting and a great challenge, spending hours drawing up plans, sifting through paperwork, creating the business neither of us could have dreamt we'd be able to pull off. A lot of hard work and kicking Robert up the bum to get him motivated went on in that home, and I have so many happy memories. Shopping with Cheryl was fun. We'd come home with a swag of new clothes and I'd do a fashion parade swirling around for Robert. All he could say was, 'How much was that?' I'd reply, 'A packet of smokes.' Or 'A carton of beer.' Never telling him the cost. For all his vices, Robert was a lovely man, and when we separated years later it was purely on good terms. I had no idea at the time how much angst and pain this company would cause me, and how it would splinter my family and cause irreparable damage. But I'll talk about that later.

One afternoon Robert and I were sitting in the garden, outside our little rental unit. His newspaper was spread out in front of his face, his big hands thumbing the pages one by one. We spent a lot of time out there, sitting like that. He then put his newspaper down and said, 'Look, there's a little unit just round the corner from here.' I peered over at the advert, curious at what he was thinking. It looked nice enough so, true to character, I said, 'Okay, let's go and have a look!'

He folded away his newspaper, I slipped on my shoes and we went around that day. I remember it was Good Friday, just before Easter. All it took was one quick look around and I bought it. It was clearly so much nicer than our current place, and I could afford the deposit myself. Again, I made sure everything was in my name, all the accounts linking back to me. He didn't argue. He knew that this was the best idea. We ended up staying in that house for seven years. He did get upset sometime later when he applied for a Visa credit card. 'It's like I don't exist!' he moaned. His name wasn't on anything, no bills, phones, cars. He was like a ghost in the eyes of the banks.

Looking into the future, seven years later, a lot had changed. Robert and I had just taken a trip overseas and were walking along the bay, peering into the estate agents' windows. We weren't looking to buy anywhere new, but I've always been impulsive with property. An agent was standing outside one shop and started telling us about this new place that had just come up on the market down in Lota. I told him we weren't interested but his slick tongue and smooth manner somehow convinced us to drive up and take a look. In true style, I took one look around the house and said, 'I'll take it.' I didn't even open a single drawer, I just knew it was the one.

Robert was slightly alarmed. 'Really?' he asked. But my mind was set. This was in 2013 and I still live in that house today, ten years later. It cost me $415,000. Again, I made sure everything was in my name alone. By this point Robert had no funds to pay half but he contributed to the mortgage payments. I was convinced this time risking losing everything again would have broken me. I couldn't do that to myself. I wouldn't be dragged down.

By this point it was only a matter of time before we split up. When we finally made the call in 2018 and decided to go our separate ways, it was amicable. We still talk to this day. He checks in on me, I go to him if I have a problem. It works much better this way. We divorced on April Fool's Day 2019.

When we broke up, I said he could keep the house because I knew I could survive whereas he would have difficulty. He refused. He packed up his little caravan and went travelling instead, all across Australia. So instead, I gave him half the value at the time, $250,000. We walked through the house together, looking at everything we'd accumulated over our years. We'd lost so much and won it all back again, over and over again. I told him to take whatever he wanted; after all, we'd spent so much of our lives together with so little, I wasn't attached to much anymore. After that he left.

I have to say it was bad timing. I knew our relationship had run its course, but everything else in my life was changing too. It was at this time that problems with Ivy began, sprouting up from the cracks, slowly splintering my life in two yet again.

Chapter 11

Developing an immunity

In 1993 I got a phone call from Max, telling me that he couldn't cope with the child anymore and she was hurtling through the sky on a plane to Australia right now. I placed the receiver down quietly and sat down. My mouth was dry, my ears rushing. I took a deep breath, trying to calm myself, but it only made the room spin. I had been waiting, fighting, for this for so long. After six long years, Ivy was finally coming home to me.

A lot of time had passed, so I knew things would be different, that it would take a while to get used to. But the seed of hope had been planted and was growing through my body, taking root as I dreamt of what we would talk about, things we might do, places we might visit. I was excited for Ruby and Jeffery to get their sibling back. Of course, I worried about Jeffery, not knowing yet how much his mental health might cope with the reunion after four years as Ivy was a bit of a mystery.

I know it was tough for Ivy. She barely had any memories of her life in Australia and although Max wasn't a great father, it's still hard leaving everything you know, especially at her age. She hadn't seen Ruby in years. It was like being adopted by distant relatives who you know exist but only as a story, an idea of some far-off family on the other side of the world.

Their first couple of weeks with me were challenging. I'd missed them with all my being, but they were nervous, confused and adjusting slowly. I knew I had to give it time. I myself was remembering how to be their mother again. Ivy was such an independent girl. Back in England she'd been running the household for years, doing her own washing, cleaning, cooking. But in other ways she seemed so young. One of the first meals we all had together, we sat around our little kitchen table, the weight of the occasion suspended in the evening light. Ruby picked up her cutlery and began cutting into her food, followed by Robert. I picked at my plate, too anxious to eat much, and caught Ivy staring at her knife and fork. Her eyebrows contorted, scrunched up together as she carefully picked up the silver utensils. She balanced them in each hand glancing over at Ruby, who was oblivious, and mimicked her actions. With a sudden jolt, I realised she didn't know how to hold the cutlery. I let her figure it out, not wanting to draw any attention to it, but inside I was shocked. Then I realised that she couldn't cut her meat with a knife and Robert helped her with it. What had Max been doing all these years? That was a pointless question in itself; of course he hadn't been doing anything.

The next few weeks trickled by. Robert was still working in the prison, and I had taken stress leave so was home to see how she was and how school was. I just wanted to restore our bond. I suppose things never work out how you want them to though. It was clear she preferred Robert to me. That was okay, I could wait for her to learn to love me again, to realise that I had not abandoned her with Max all those years ago, that I'd been pining for her ever since. But it just didn't ever quite get there.

She got on well with her brother and even through all his

breakdowns they would talk, stay in contact. Her teenage years passed by in an uneventful haze. My hopes of rekindling our relationship slowly fizzled, leaving an amicable but tense empty space in its place. I was just never quite sure how to be around her. When she felt upset or hurt, she would hold on to it. Ruby and Jeffery always got on well and I'm sure this only heightened the difference with Ivy. I never wanted her to feel left out, but maybe all those years in England really did drive an unbreakable wedge between us. Maybe her feelings of abandonment were just too deep to be able to repair.

She was almost nineteen when she moved out to live with her boyfriend, Murray. For the next few years we just lived our lives quietly, separately but with no bad feelings. I wished we were closer, but I had no idea what I was getting into. Eventually, around 2011, she started working for me. This was the beginning of the end. If I had known how she could be, I would have kept her far away.

Chapter 12

The company

A hard won defeat.

I don't hate my daughter, but I think she's done some unkind things. Not just to me, but to our family, to her family, to the people we looked after together and the people that we've let down. It takes a lot of energy to dislike someone, and I'm getting too tired for that now. So I don't waste my time anymore. I won't let her ruin my life again.

Since 2001 I had been working for Autism Queensland. I'd graduated from the welfare course with my diploma and sailed straight into working for Autism Queensland at a house at Wellington Point. I absolutely adored this job. It was working with three autistic ladies, looking after them in a government funded supported home. The place was beautiful – each bedroom had an ensuite and the staff bedroom office was cosy. My job was essentially that of a mother. Each morning at nine o'clock they would leave for the day to go to the support centre. I'd pack their lunches, send them off and then make sure that the house was ready for when they returned home. I would get their dinner ready, do their washing and their ironing. I've always enjoyed doing washing, so this really was a strangely perfect job for me. I worked with these women for over nineteen years.

All three women were non-verbal, so I ended up doing a lot of the talking. Essentially it was what I'd been doing my entire life, looking after people. But this time I was getting paid and the people I cared for appreciated my efforts. Instead of being met with a violent outburst if I burnt the toast, I was greeted with gratitude for making a new slice. Instead of being treated as an impromptu therapist for deeply psychiatrically damaged murderers, I was listened to all day, able to solve the small problems such as how to get a stain out of a blouse. It may sound mundane but every day I knew I was making these women's lives so much better. I could see their joy in my presence. No matter how small the victories were, each one felt special.

When Robert started the company, we took over the house from Autism Queensland. He also took over the house he had done his placement in. Those first few years were so exciting, so new. If I'd been told it would snowball into the multimillion-dollar business it became, I would have never believed it.

By 2011 we had expanded to own three houses, each one housing a number of clients we cared for and a sizeable amount of staff looking after them. It had been a difficult three years, papering over the cracks in Robert's and my relationship, dealing with Jeff's ever declining mental health and trying to recover from our financial troubles. But we did it. The days of sleeping in Sheryl's basement were over. When Kerry said she wanted to separate from the business, to go out on her own, we were supportive. Of course it meant splitting the assets, working out which clients would stay with us and which would go to her new venture, but I knew this was what I wanted to do with my life, so it would be worth it.

It turned out to be a lot more charged than I expected. It began amicably, with one of our houses opting to stay with Kerry and the other two deciding to stick with Robert and me. I was pleased, as it's always heartwarming to be recognised as good at what you do, and this was proof that our clients really did want to stay with us. Robert's son, Kevin, was working in one of the houses she ran. He had just left the navy and was looking for something to do while he found his feet. It seemed Kerry wasn't happy with leaving with just one house; she wanted another. So one afternoon she came to Robert and told him that he needed to hand over the rights to another house. He refused. So then she dropped a bombshell on him. She told him that if he didn't let her take this house then she would tell the department that his son Kevin had behaved inappropriately with one of the clients. Robert was stunned. His mouth dropped open, and he stood there, his eyes glazed over, staring past Kerry.

After that conversation he wasn't himself for a long time. The mere suggestion had horrified him, cut some part of him so deeply that he needed to physically leave Brisbane in order to recover. He barely ate, barely slept, wouldn't even get up some days. I was overcome with anxiety. Stress became my newest companion, shrouding the days in a prickling pressure, ready to overflow any minute. I needed Robert to help with the separation of the company, needed his mind sharp, but he was incapable. I had to call the shots and all he could do was sign on the dotted line. Eventually I sent him up to Darwin, to stay with his daughter. She sorted him out, gave him the reassurance he needed. It did him good to get away.

Back in Brisbane, I was under a lot of pressure. I'd been with the company since the beginning, knew it better than anyone, but I needed help. This was where Ivy came in. She'd been working in a law firm in the city in human resources and had just had her first child, Hudson. Since Hudson was born, I was always helping out, doing washing, housework, and cooking their tea. I love being a grandmother. Shortly after he was born,

I was at Ivy's house in her kitchen, helping out with some odd jobs. I was at the sink, my elbows deep in soapy water, when I turned to her and said, 'I'm going to be a better grandmother than I was a mother.' Hudson was propped on her hip, slowly being rocked back and forth. But once I'd said that she stopped, staring directly at me. A look I couldn't quite pinpoint appeared on her face and I knew that it had really touched her.

I really needed to get some help with the company and Ivy offered. Every morning on her train journey into the city she would fill out the paperwork, carefully going over the endless documents and contracts. It was a relief to have someone to share the logistics with, someone who also knew about the paperwork behind a business. But the more she helped out with the company, the more I ended up helping her out at home. I would spend the day searching for new properties, setting them up from scratch, furnishing them, finding staff, organising wi-fi: all the mundane daily tasks. But then I'd come home and go straight to Ivy's, cook her kids' dinner, and wait for whatever tradie while she was at work. I loved spending time with my grandson, but it felt like I was working two jobs. I didn't realise it at the time, but I was gradually being squeezed out of the company's operations and sidelined.

This carried on for two years until 2013, when Ivy had Casey and left her job at the law firm to work full-time at my company. When Robert returned from Darwin he had gone back to working on the floor. No matter how much needed doing in the office, we both wanted to spend as much time in the homes, working with our clients. This was why we had started the company, because we both genuinely loved being able to help people. Naturally, Ivy saw this as an opportunity to take on more work in the office. She said she would help us out, take over the wages from me so we didn't have to worry about that anymore. I was grateful for the help, so of course we said yes.

It was my open heart that truly lost me the company. I trusted Ivy, she was my daughter. But this turned out to be my downfall. In 2015 she asked me for shares in the company. Robert was still the founder but by this time my official title was director. I didn't really want him to give us the shares, but Ivy was always there, whispering in my ear. She said that we needed them, that it was only right after all the hard work we'd both put in. I would repeat this back to Robert, his face a jigsaw of confusion at my change of tack. He knew shares didn't bother me, but I didn't stop asking. She wouldn't let me stop. Eventually Robert had enough and made us both shareholders, giving us ten each. But this wasn't enough for her.

I can't pinpoint when the abuse began. It must have started small, growing, shifting into vile spewing of expletives fired my way. She would belittle me, call me names, chisel down at my self-esteem that I had spent years repairing after her father left. I felt so low, so deflated. I was always walking on eggshells around her. She would threaten to take the company away, take the clients and start her own business. But worse than that was when she would threaten to take away my grandchildren, stop me from seeing them. I slowly retreated into myself. Outwardly I tried as hard as possible to be the same chatty woman, going about my job, moving through the motions. But inside I was heartbroken, sinking into a grey depression. The rage that had propelled me through all those years with Max had softened into meek sadness. I didn't have the fire left to fight her, I just wanted peace, but I felt nothing.

Over the years she'd slowly risen up through the company. She shouted the loudest, put on the best front, while I worked on the floor, running things behind the scenes. But a lot of the staff thought she was the boss. Especially the newer people. They had no idea that I had set the company up with Robert all those years ago. They only saw me perched behind the reception desk, a smile waiting for them each morning.

In 2017 at Christmas Ivy flew back to England to see her father. I was grateful for the respite, though I feared what would await upon her return. Sadly, I was right to be worried. When she arrived back, a new venom ran through her and she spurted hurtful torrents of abuse, her belittling attacks smattering my days. These would be peppered with periods of complete radio silence, as she retreated, leaving me feeling confused, unaware of what was happening and worthless. I never knew what was coming next, what she would use against me to say I'd done wrong. I wasn't eating or sleeping but held out hope. She knew she had complete control over me, knew that I would do anything to see her boys.

Her biggest assault came in January 2018. She wanted more shares, but Robert was standing his ground. She couldn't quite manipulate him in the same way she could me. For years she'd been begging me to leave him, citing his gambling and drinking as the reasons. Robert was far from perfect and these were indeed his flaws, but they were not the reason she wanted him to leave. She knew that once he was out of the picture, it would be far easier for her to access the company and its remaining assets.

So she accused Robert of molesting her. After what happened with Kevin, she knew this was the way to get to him, knew he would do anything to clear his name. And she was right. While she worked on destroying Robert, she continued to hurt me. Her insults became nastier, more targeted. I'd go to her house to see the children and she'd drop into conversation that so and so at work hated me, thinks I'm stupid. Every insecurity, every minor anxiety she picked up on, she would use it against us. She knew the shame I carried about my lack of education, my inability to write over the years, and used this to her advantage.

Crying became my daily practice, weeping in the car, in the toilets at work, at home alone. She moved her tormenting outside of the house, bringing it into work, packed it into her bag with her lunch. She would fling these barbed comments at me in front of other members of staff, even clients. Each arrow would sink deep into my heart, burying themselves in a graveyard of lost connection. Towards the end I would wake up lying in bed, and for a few seconds feel okay. The sleepy haze of the early morning light would filter through the window, the sweet smell of daybreak relaxing my tense body. But it was only ever a few seconds. Then I would remember –remember my life and everything it encompassed. My eyes would shut, a heavy cloak dropping over my limbs as I forced myself to get out of bed, dragging myself through another agonising day. I longed for the moment I would get to climb back into bed and feel nothing again.

I considered killing myself. It felt like being trapped under Max's spell all over again. But this time there wasn't a way out. I would never stop trying to see my grandchildren, I knew that. As long as she wanted something from me, she would never stop. And I had the feeling that she would always want something from me.

Eventually, it all became too much and Robert's and my relationship broke down. It was a culmination of things. Robert had begun to live outside on the back patio with his fridge, big Foxtel TV, kitchen table and chair, and his use of cigarettes increased. He would come into the house, cook a meal and take it back outside to eat despite me pleading for him to eat with me or sit in when family visited.

It was around this time that I pushed Robert into giving me

and Ivy some more of his shares. Of course, Ivy had her own agenda. She would switch between charm and attack, giving and taking at colossal speed. She was the good cop and the bad cop, leaving me exhausted in our negotiations. It hurt to see her using her family as leverage, refusing to let me see her kids if I didn't cooperate. She'd call me up and say, 'If you don't come and get these kids I'm going to fucking kill them!' So of course I would go. I'd do anything for those children. It felt like I was nineteen again, dropping everything to protect my family from an abusive person. Only this time it wasn't my husband, it was my daughter. Eventually Robert refused to give her any more shares so I gave her mine.

After the accusations, she and Robert weren't speaking, so I became the go-between, hastily trying to patch up our disintegrating relationship. When the final conversation unfolded, it was one of exasperation. She'd bullied and forced her way in and wasn't about to back down. She'd push me further and further, knowing full well that I just wanted this to be over. I said I would take fifty-one per cent of the shares and she could have forty-nine. Robert had originally had sixty, so that was still far more than she had previously owned. But that wasn't enough. She said we have to go fifty–fifty so that the accountant can calculate the dividends properly. In a snap of frustration, I agreed to fifty–fifty. I had a sinking feeling in my stomach as I signed the contract, but I pushed it away. I just wanted the fighting to end. It was probably one of the stupidest and biggest mistakes I've ever made in my life. But, at the time, I felt that I had little or no choice.

She sacked me on the 6th of September 2019. Throughout everything, she had always said, 'Mum, I'll always look after you.' Now it was impossible to even pretend this might be true. From March she had been cutting my pay, lowering my wages so much that I couldn't even afford to buy a cup of coffee out in a cafe. I was back on my three-dollar meal plans, batch cooking and freezing everything for the week. I was broken emotionally, lonely and desperate.

Without my work and without Robert to distract me, my world had become very small. I was stuck in a sinkhole of despair, shocked that my own daughter seemed to enjoy making me feel this way. The dance I'd been doing with depression finally gave over, and I sank into its grey embrace. Sleeping became my only escape, I barely ate, I had no reason to look after myself. Soon even the thought of seeing my grandchildren wasn't enough to rouse me.

I called Robert. After the split he had packed up his van and gone travelling across the country. At this point he was out in Sydney. I was a wreck, sobbing these huge tears, my despair trickling down the phone line, streaming across the country. 'I'm going to go to the office, pour petrol over myself and burn,' I told Robert. It wasn't a cry for attention; in that moment I fully meant it. He laughed. 'No you're not, don't be silly,' he replied. 'Ivy will just come out and start toasting marshmallows on you.' A dry cackle escaped my lips. I coughed, swallowing tears and spitting laughter as I sucked in the air. It was then that I knew I would be okay, that I could get through this.

I sued my own company for unfair dismissal. There was no other way, I needed the money. Ivy wanted the company for herself, but she also wanted to create her own. She needed clients and staff, so decided it would just be easier to take the ones we already had. In November I spoke to my lawyers. It was clear the company was going to go into liquidation. It hurt so much seeing this incredible thing that Robert and I had built over the years be tainted, cut up and bled dry. Ivy had attached herself like a leech, sucking out the life, drop by drop.

After she'd sacked me, and unbeknown to me, she immediately increased the input into building her own company, registering it in late September. She just needed a bit more time to finalise the details. I had a liquidation court date on the 7th of December, and she panicked. It was too soon. If the company went under now, she wouldn't be ready to open her new business. So she stalled, paying me some of the wages she owed me. But it was only a ploy for more time. I originally put the company into liquidation, but I then halted the process because I thought we might be working things out. Ivy then used my application papers without my permission to finally put the company into liquidation in the winter of 2020. On Tuesday morning it went to court and by two o'clock that afternoon the liquidators were in the offices, stripping them bare. Her new company was up and running that very week. Needless to say, I was completely gobsmacked.

A lot of the staff had remained loyal to her. She'd played so many others the same way she'd played me. If she needed something from them, she knew exactly what to say, what to do. But as soon as her use for them was over, it was like they did not exist. Some of them had abandoned me during the whole debacle but over the coming months some would drop back into my life, feeding me new bits of information, telling me the latest dramatic turn of events.

She had told so many untruths. It was hurtful to hear her badmouthing me to so many people we knew. They were informed that I had left her in England with Max on purpose when she was young, that I never wanted to bring her to Australia. That cut me deeply. I feel that she sometimes has difficulty recognising reality from fiction. So much of her whole existence is based on her odd perspectives on life.

I was surprised by how much media attention the case got. Newspapers, journalists, local news, the lot, they all wanted to speak with me. I complied with a few, as it helped to get my story out there. I faced abuse online as well. Strangers on the internet called me a bad mother, a selfish woman. They said that Ivy was a good person and would never try to hurt anyone on purpose. It was clear to them that I was the bad guy and she was the victim. Since I'd scraped myself away from the drudgery of depression, I have rekindled the burning anger that had been buried deep inside me. But I wasn't the same as I used to be and I wasn't going to fight back. What good would it do? So I stopped going online, stopped listening to strangers trapped behind keyboards, tapping away about people they'd never met and never would.

The whole thing cost me a fortune. I knew it was necessary but after the legal fees I wasn't left with anywhere near as much as I'd hoped. By April 2021, I'd had to get a new lawyer. After years of gaslighting I was so unsure of my own judgement so that I had to get my family to vet them for me, to check that I was making good, informed decisions. I wasn't about to be screwed over again. Ruby, John, Carol and Rand would all sit and ask questions, gathered around the table, notepad in hand. They really helped me get through this.

Then the pandemic hit, and I was swept up into another whirlwind. Living alone I wouldn't speak to anyone for weeks at a time. Robert was still checking in on me, making sure I was okay. Despite everything, we really have ended up as good friends.

I ran into Ivy for the first time since the dispute in November 2022. I was at Murray's, her ex-husband's house, playing football in the garden with the boys. The sun was shining and we were messing about, their legs blurring together as they weaved in and out, slipping the ball between each other. I was laughing, enjoying spending time outside with them. She appeared in front of the garage and stopped in her tracks. Hudson ran up to her, grabbing a bag from her still hands. 'Thanks, Mum!' he chirped, skirting away. She was dropping off some forgotten homework and hadn't realised I was going to be there. We stood in silence, just looking at one another. Then she left. Seeing her was cathartic. I realised that she can't hurt me anymore and that I had been true to myself through the entire disgusting affair.

That was it. That moment had been built up in my head to be so much worse, but it was just empty. I didn't feel any way towards her anymore, of which in a certain sense I'm glad. I don't want to let her take any more of my life from me. That being said, I don't want her at my funeral.

Chapter 13

Friendship and family

The good and the bad

Sheryl was my best friend and she was also Robert's sister. She had split up with her husband in 1994, moving in with me and Robert shortly after. She was great fun, always laughing and joking. The years she was with us were difficult, but she added more light than she created darkness. Like Robert, she was a gambler so I suppose it ran in the family.

She even worked with us at the company, in one of the homes, starting around 2009. She worked on the floor, looking after the clients, but also in the office, handling paperwork, filing. She was an excellent employee, and ambitious too. After a while she came to us with a proposition. She wanted to open a day branch, a service for the clients that would allow them to partake in activities or go on trips. She had dreams of organising drawing classes, cooking workshops, and financial seminars. I thought this was a wonderful idea. It would really give us the edge over our competitors and improve the quality of our clients' care significantly.

At this point I was still at the company. Ivy had yet to do her damage and we were working well as a team. So Ivy, Sheryl and I set up 'Bayside Basement', a day-care branch. This was separate to Robert and the main company, at Ivy's insistence. I guess that should have been a warning. But it was brilliant seeing Sheryl thrive like this. She had her own staff, her own team and she ran it so well.

However, despite our closeness it sometimes felt like Sheryl took advantage of me. A certain look would pass over her face when we were sitting together, and I just knew what she was going to ask me. It was always about money. All those years I was a rock for her and Robert, their lighthouse in the chaotic storm. The problem was, she genuinely always needed it. By the time she had to ask me, it was already a last resort. Without my intervention, the power in her daughter's house would be cut off or she wouldn't be able to feed her kids that week. She knew I wouldn't say no, but I could tell it hurt her to have to ask.

Every time I hoped it would be the last time. But the problem with addicts is that it never is. They will always push and push and push until something snaps completely. She always paid me back, though, often not on time, but always in the end. That was something at least. Our friendship wasn't one of equals. Of course, we got on so well, supporting each other emotionally, being a heart to turn to, but when one of you has the financial power, it will never be quite solid.

It hurts that money played a part in the disintegration of our friendship. I needed her to be there for me, but she just wasn't. It was after I'd been sacked from the company, in 2019, when I went over to her new unit. I'd been calling her on the phone but there was no answer. She'd been leaving my texts unread and emails unanswered. I was confused by her sudden silence and I just wanted to talk to someone.

When I arrived, I had to slip through the big gates outside her unit. Waiting for them to grind open I felt nervous, the constant anxiety that had plagued me for the last few years churning away in my gut. When she opened the door, she had a duster in one hand, a spray bottle in the other. Ushering me in, she barely made eye contact. Frantically scrubbing at the surfaces, she twittered lightly, brushing over the pleasantries and keeping her chatter constantly going. I was confused. It wasn't normally like this. I could tell she was nervous, desperate to occupy herself so she didn't have to focus on me.

Eventually I pierced a hole in her veil of chatter. 'Why are you doing this?' I asked, a palpable sadness choking my words. She didn't stop cleaning, avoiding my wavering gaze and continuing to polish the spotless countertop. She mumbled back, 'Oh, you've caused a lot of trouble ...' Trailing off she began to half-heartedly list the things that had taken a turn since Ivy's dissolution of the company. Worried parents calling up about their children's safety, the idea that Robert and I were a threat and incapable of caring for the residents. I swallowed, a thick lump rising in my throat. I could tell she wasn't going to give, to be able to help me. I felt weak, completely alone.

Now that Robert was gone, Ruby became my rock. Trying to explain what Ivy had done, that I had been completely manipulated, bullied and coerced into decisions I did not agree with was difficult, but Ruby was there to listen. I doubted even my own judgement. It had been going on for years, starting so subtly but eroding my confidence day by day, until I was just a husk of a human being.

Sheryl was well aware how low I was, that I couldn't pay my mortgage, couldn't afford to eat properly. But if she had listened to me, just sat down and stopped for a second, I would have told her. I suppose that's why she didn't want to know, as this way she could convince herself that I was fine, maybe hard done by, but ultimately would land on my feet.

All I wanted was to talk to her, to sit and for her to listen. The rejection stung me, cut right to my core. Vulnerability wrapped itself around me, choking me as I stood there, inwardly retreating. I realised she wasn't going to be there for me. But I took a deep breath, stood up tall and asked, 'So, are we good though?' 'Yeah of course,' was her reply. Although, as I walked out of her little rental unit, my back to her, I knew this wasn't true.

As expected, after this she ignored me. Even though I knew it was coming, it still hurt, so I decided to go back, to try one final time. It didn't make a difference. She was even more agitated and could barely sit still. After that I knew it would be the last time I would try. I wasn't going to force her to be my friend. Despite everything, I had more respect than that. This happened just before the company crumbled. She could see the way it was going and realised that her days of working there were numbered.

She ended up with a $38,000 payout for leaving the business. Apparently she'd told Ivy that she was involved in setting up the company in the early days, so had demanded more. Sheryl was always good at getting what she wanted. After that she left Brisbane, moving down to Sydney to be with her mother. I heard it was only meant to be a visit, but Robert said once she arrived, she just never left. Their mother was sick, so she stayed to look after her. I hope she managed better down there, built a new life for herself.

Robert had another sister, Jenny. I didn't know her as well as Sheryl, but I still liked her. It was months later that Robert mentioned that Sheryl's granddaughter was getting married but neither Sheryl nor Jenny were going, as they didn't want to leave their mother. She was too sick to travel. So, I volunteered to go down and look after her. They were all slightly taken aback, after how Sheryl and I had left things. We weren't exactly speaking. But I had always had a soft spot for their mother – she was a good woman – so I was more than happy to do it. After a brief hesitation they agreed, flying down to Melbourne for the wedding while I stayed in Sydney. This happened a couple more times over the coming months and though I can't say it was easy, I enjoyed spending time with their mother.

But the last time I travelled down to help, I felt uncomfortable. I could see Jenny was uneasy with me being there, and Sheryl in true form followed suit, mirroring her discomfort. I decided this would be my last trip. It only seemed fair. That was the thing with Sheryl, she always needed someone to look after her. I remember Robert once saying that she was a user, not in a cruel way, it was just how it was. She always needed someone and for years I had mistaken that reliance for friendship. Now Jenny held that position, and in all honesty, once I realised, I was okay with that. Once their mother died, I knew she was going to stay there.

I went to the funeral. It felt like the right thing to do and I wanted to pay my respects. Their mother had been good to me and I was always grateful for that. After the service I got a call from my sister, Cindy. I wasn't sure why she was calling me, but it was not the reason I expected. Her son Lorr had hanged himself. He was only twenty-six. I was devastated. I knew how low you have to be to think that's the only way out. I couldn't imagine what Cindy was going through. Things with Jeff had been bad but at least I still had him, he'd never fully committed himself to his demons.

I told Sheryl and she stared at me, blurting out, 'That's just selfish!' I was stunned. I knew tensions were high as we were at her own mother's funeral, but this was not what I expected from her at all, after all these years. I was furious, my words spitting back like hot sparks. I told her she had no idea how it feels to be that low, that desperate that your pain swallows you whole, bottling your vision, leaving no room to think of anyone else's feelings or pain. Being that depressed makes you unable to see past yourself, trapped in your own temple of misery.

We'd never had an argument before, so she'd never seen this venom directed at her. Now it was her turn to be stunned. Swallowing, she mumbled something under her breath, made her excuses and left. I'm not usually a confrontational person but that really hurt me. I know what it's like to feel that way, that the only way out is death. My failed attempts back in Wellingborough and my suicidal thoughts after the dispute still burned strong inside of me. Some things I just can't shake.

That was the last time I ever saw Sheryl. It still makes me sad to this day. I don't want to tarnish the golden memories we had over all those years but when I look back now, they feel almost dirty, like she was just using me. I hope I'm wrong, that hindsight has swayed me.

My biggest fear was always that I would end up like my mother: being completely broke, living in Housing Commission accommodation and dying alone. She died in March 2022. Jim had passed away before her, unexpectedly, of cancer. They had both been terrible with money and had lost their house, moving back into rentals. Once it was just my mother left, her pension wasn't enough to support herself. In the end, Cindy and I used to subsidise her rent and shopping, and I'd buy her bulk meat.

Once she was moved into Housing Commission accommodation, she had slightly more freedom. They only charge a quarter of your income for rent, so this gave her some leeway to enjoy her final years. But this scared the shit out of me. She was 17,000 kilometres across the world, but in the exact same position that she'd been born into: living in a council house, with no money and nothing to her name. I know I am not my mother, but I'm always afraid of slipping back down there, back to the cold streets of London, those dark days of Wellingborough.

My family has always had secrets. I had my own fair share, of course. But my brother Michael had far more. In 2017, he was arrested for downloading child pornography onto his computer. He was living in a house with his son and grandson, when the police knocked on his door. Mark, his son, opened the door to them. 'You've been transferring files containing indecent images of underage children,' they accused. Mark panicked. 'No, I haven't,' he said, horror spreading across his face. Apparently, it was at this point that Michael emerged, raised his hands above his head and said, 'No, it was me.' They found over five thousand images on his computer.

That was the end of that relationship. I was driving when Cindy told me. Michael and I had never really been close. Even when he was younger, he'd exhibited some uncomfortable behaviours. When I first moved out to Australia and lived in my mother's garage with Max, I'd seen him reach around my mother and touch her breasts. She was unconcerned by this, shrugging him off and shooing him away. It made me deeply uncomfortable. Another time, he'd come home drunk from a night out and was sitting in the living room. I woke up in the morning, traipsing through and saw him naked form the waist down, touching himself. I was shocked, quickly leaving the room, disgusted with what I witnessed. But my mother had already been in the room ironing. There's no way she couldn't see what he was doing. It was horribly inappropriate, vile behaviour.

After he was released from jail, I never spoke to him again. He'd only been sentenced to eight months but served four. Four months, that was it. It makes me sick just thinking about it. He didn't tell our mother, in fact no one did. We didn't want to think about him, let alone give him air time. Eventually we couldn't put off her questioning any further. She'd ask why he hadn't called her recently and we'd reply that he was away on a camping trip or taking a holiday. I'm sure she didn't believe us.

So one afternoon, Carol, Cindy and I went over to our mother's apartment. We'd decided we needed to tell her as a group, but once we walked into her house a heavy silence fell. The air was stale, the atmosphere thin. Taking a deep breath, I realised I was going to have to do this myself. Being the oldest always meant the difficult conversations fell to me. So I just spat it out. 'Oh right,' she uttered.

My mother has always lived in denial, it's how she managed to get through life feeling so guiltless about the people she's hurt. I could see her brain ticking over, working out the best way to bury this new knowledge deep into her subconscious, so it would never have to see the light again. That was that. I know she continued her relationship with him, and I didn't care about it.

Michael died of a heart attack in August 2020. This time it was a call from my mother. I felt nothing. A few minutes later Cindy called, told me the details: that he'd collapsed at work, his colleagues gave him CPR but it wasn't enough. Apparently he kept just repeating, 'Please, let me go!' His last words echoed through my mind for days.

My mother took his ashes after the funeral. Before she died, she called us all up, her three daughters, and asked who would take his ashes after she died. She knew she didn't have long left and wanted to make sure someone looked after him. I was revolted, told her that if it were up to me, they were going straight down the toilet. Needless to say, I wasn't the chosen recipient. Cindy took him and then gave them to his best friend.

My mother died on the 10th of March 2022 of cancer, when she was eighty-six years old. I felt absolutely nothing. No grief, no sadness, not even loss. I'd spent more time with her in my adult life than I could ever have dreamt of as a child, but I never forgave her for what she did to me when I was young. I cared for her in those last years, when she had lost everything, but it was out of duty, not love. Honestly, I think I've spent my whole life compartmentalising. If I allowed myself to truly feel, I'm not sure I would be able to cope. A lot of people whom I loved and who were supposed to love me, ended up betraying me and I'm not sure I could bear to fully understand how this has affected me. So it's much easier to box it off, keep it hidden. Maybe one day I'll let it all out, but not yet.

During her last year, I got the chance to finally ask my mother the questions that I'd been sitting on my whole life. But I didn't get the answers I hoped for. Carol and I went to her when she was ill, knowing that we'd regret not speaking to her properly if we didn't. The pain of our childhood still lingered; it had shaped us into the people we are today, and we wanted to know why she was the way she was.

I expected lightning, thunder. But it turned out to be quite the opposite. Sylvia was one of thirteen children and had a normal, comfortable upbringing. Then of course the war started, and she was evacuated, split up from her brothers and sisters, never fully reunited. She remained with one of her sisters in a children's home, but she said the worst punishment she ever had was cleaning. In all honesty, I'm not sure if she was telling the truth, but for her sake I hope she was. It doesn't explain the way she treated us, the violence and abuse she imposed, but I've had a long time to come to terms with that.

I remember one afternoon, a long time ago, she went with me to visit Jeffery at Wolston Park. As we walked through the gates, down the narrow corridors, our shoes squeaking on the polished floors, she shuddered. I only saw it out of the corner of my eye, but I could see her glancing around, shifting from foot to foot, discomfort seeping out of her like from an oozing wound. 'I have to get out of here,' she said quietly. I think it brought back bad memories. It's funny though, she had no problems leaving me in a home when I was a teenager.

I'd often try to forget my childhood. The memories are still painful, they still feel so raw. But as anyone who's had a traumatic past knows, it's impossible to fully escape. Christmas is always hard. As much as I try to forget, I always circle back to one year when I was around thirteen. My mother and Bob had been out Christmas shopping all day. Carol and I were at home, thinking about what they might have bought for us. We were poor, but we always got a present. I heard the slam of the front door opening, the rattle of the key in the frosted lock. The cackle of loud voices as my mother and Bob entered the room. I sat around the corner, out of their line of sight. 'Wait!' my mother's voice rang out, 'We forgot Susan.' I felt desolate. It wasn't that they couldn't find anything for me, that they didn't know me well enough to know what I wanted. I had been completely forgotten, and that was far worse.

During the years in Wellingborough it didn't get any better. For so many years of my life I never received a single gift. So, without fail, I would go to the shops and buy myself a packet of thin mints, wrap them up and place them under the tree. There was always a flicker of hope that there might be something else, but there never was. I wouldn't let myself feel the shame, the aching little girl inside. I still do it to this day. It's become my ritual. It used to help me keep up the facade that I was living a normal life, that I was part of a functioning family. But now I do it to remind myself that even in the darkest moments, I was always trying to create some joy, to find some happiness. I like remembering it that way.

Many years later I was up in Darwin with Robert for Christmas. I must have been around sixty-one. People kept sneaking glances at me, whispering in hushed tones. I was perplexed, so asked Robert what they were talking about. He said that they thought I was getting confused, that I might have Alzheimer's. I was shocked. I felt completely normal, completely myself. But for so many people to have clocked something, I figured I might as well see a doctor, just to check.

I made an appointment with the doctor, who referred me to a neurologist. After a number of scans and tests, he cleared me of any degenerative diseases but asked if I had experienced any trauma as a child. Slowly, I nodded. He explained there was very limited blood flow to my prefrontal cortex, suggesting some sort of physical or even mental incident in my developing years. A dull memory tugged at the corners of my consciousness. My mother's hands, full of fistfuls of hair, mine and Carol's, smashing our skulls together. Bruises the size of plums, capillaries bursting like dams, red blotting ink soaking across the sides of our heads. I pushed it away, left the doctor's and went home. I didn't follow up; I didn't need another diagnosis. This is the way I am, the way I have always been, and I was not going to change it.

It was after my mother's funeral that one of my own secrets came out. I take pride in owning up to mistakes when I've been in the wrong. Unfortunately, this is one of the times that I've been selfish and I've hurt people. So here's what happened.

First, I want to say that I've always been there for Carol. When we were younger, of course we would fight, but as adults she'd been there for me in times of need and vice versa. In 2019 she and Rand got into a pretty serious car accident. They had been on holiday to New South Wales and were driving home. They puttered to a stop at some roadworks, waiting for the lights to flash so they could go on. But while they waited, out of nowhere a huge truck roared down the road, smashing into them at eighty kilometres an hour.

That could have been it for them. They both had cracked spines and were carted off to Lismore hospital immediately. When I got the call to say they'd been in an accident, my blood ran cold. It felt like I'd been smacked, my stomach twisting and wrenching as I processed the tinny words tumbling down the phone. I immediately packed a bag, called Ruby and her husband, John, and drove down to see them. The whole drive I felt sick. I wasn't prepared to lose Carol. I needed her in my life. When we finally arrived, they looked awful, their bodies crimson and navy, bruises blossoming across their fragile skin. Their weakness emanated from their plastic beds, their frail hands cool between my palms. My heart ached seeing her like this.

But this wasn't the event that was going to separate us, although I didn't realise at the time, the damage had already been done. It was just waiting to be unveiled at the right moment. Over the coming days and weeks, I drove up to visit them, bringing them clothes or toiletries, anything they needed, or I thought might help. Eventually, once they were well enough to be moved, I took them back home. Cruising down the open roads, I drove carefully, hyper-aware of their situation, doing my best to take each corner slowly, to avoid any bumps in the tattered tarmac.

They had a long road to recovery. Carol had to wear thick back braces to keep her spine straight and both their limbs were a mess of broken bones, their brains battered, and tendons tweaked. They had so many injuries I couldn't keep track of them all. I wanted to help, to do whatever I could for them, so I would drive them to their hospital appointments. These occurred three or four times a week, so we spent a lot of time together, sometimes talking, sometimes in companionable silence. This went on for over a year.

Eventually, they both got compensation for the accident. After all, it wasn't their fault. Our relationship was strong at this point – we saw each other all the time and I looked after Carol. But after our mother died, Cindy dropped a bombshell.

In 1984 I had a fling with Rand. I'm not proud of it and regret it deeply. It was the first year I'd arrived in Australia, just after Max had left for England. He'd been teaching me to drive and we'd always got on well. At this point he and Carol were already married. It was very short-lived, a tiny fling. I had buried it in my consciousness over the years – after all it was so long ago. Deep down I'd always thought that Carol already knew. She had inherited her ability to deny the obvious from our mother.

But after Cindy told her, she was understandably heartbroken, angry and distraught. Confronting Randall, she asked if it was true, and he admitted that it was. After that she cut off all communication with me. They're still together, living just down the road. I was devastated. I knew that what I had done was awful, but she was my sister and I still needed her. I haven't seen them since. I hope that one day she can forgive me, that we can patch things up between us.

Of course, I was livid with Cindy. It wasn't her place to tell Carol at all. We used to speak on the phone every week but since then, she's kept her distance, she knows I'm still disappointed. It makes me sad that my sibling relationships have become so fractured, but I've managed to build up my own life outside of my family to keep myself fulfilled. I still don't fully understand why Cindy told her. When her son hanged himself, I was there for her. I knew what it was like to have a mentally unwell child. We went through a lot together.

Carol's son, Jason, also has mental health issues. Our family really didn't get the luck of the draw when it comes to sanity and we've all suffered at one time or another. Jason didn't leave the house. He would stay in all day, flitting around the internet on his laptop up in his bedroom. He came off his medication and that was not a good time for anyone. It would be easy to blame my mother for all this. After all, she is the one source of all our overlapping DNA.

Even now, when I'm in one of the best places I've ever been, I'm still on medication. Zoloft. I haven't ever been properly assessed but some of my behaviour leans towards bipolar. When I'm on medication, I become stable, a more relaxed version of myself. When I come off the meds, which I occasionally do, I become far more manic, almost erratic. I clean incessantly, but I've always loved cleaning, so I guess it just exacerbates it. But I'll feel on top of the world for a few weeks, where anything is possible and I have such pure enthusiasm for life, belief in myself. Then I'll plummet, my mood sinking into a pit of despair, unable to do the simplest of tasks.

One time I tried to wean myself off gradually, hoping it would work. I was elbow deep in dishwashing, the foamy bubbles slipping over my hands in the silken water. Robert was sitting on the couch in the lounge watching something on television. My mood was high and I felt like I was flying, a glorious wave of uninterrupted glee surging through my body. I looked over at him, laughed and called out, 'You know what, you want to get up off the couch, do some exercise and you might be able to see your dick and then use it!' He was completely aghast, as that was not what he expected me to say. I just cackled, getting back to the dishes.

The thing is, that is me. When I'm happy, I say what I like and I don't worry about being wrong or people disagreeing. At my core I'm an outspoken, confident woman. I've just been through so many phases of life where that's been chipped away, my edges sanded down into a diluted version. So sometimes, when I really feel like myself, I think it shocks people, they're not quite used to it.

But I also know that staying on my medication is what's best for me now. A couple of years ago I took a computer course. I love computers. I'm curious about the world and I don't want to be one of those people who are stuck living in the past. Anyway, I'd taken the course and had worked really hard, picking up the information, even teaching some of the other attendees what I'd learnt. I felt confident as this was something I was good at.

But when it came to the exam, I had begun tapering off my meds. I sat there in the bright room, the clacking of keyboards trickling in my ear drums, tapping away behind my eyeballs. Everyone else's fingers moved effortlessly across the pads, their agile fingers typing away. But I was frozen. I couldn't remember anything, my mind was full of grit, a foggy haze clouded my thoughts. Tears began to bubble in the corners of my eyes, my mind racing in a jungle of jumbled confusion. I just couldn't think straight.

Since then, I decided staying on the Zoloft was the best idea. A professional diagnosis is expensive, so for now I'm happy to just keep going on. I sometimes wonder if my childhood affected me in this way at all, if my upbringing is responsible. Or if it was hardwired into my body, programmed into me from the moment I drew my first breath. I don't know the answer, and for now that's okay.

Chapter 14

Grandchildren

A second chance to do things better

I'd never given much thought to abortion, not until I had one myself. In fact, not just one, but two. The first one right after Ivy was born, the second in my late thirties, when I was with Robert. I have no regrets about either of them. Neither time was right to bring another child into the world and I would have done them more harm than good.

My grandchildren are the lights of my life. I've always said I'll be a better nan than I was a mum. I tried my best as a mother, but I was just painfully young and ill-equipped. I couldn't be more overjoyed with the family I've created over the years. Even on Robert's side, though I don't see them anymore, I think of his children as part of my family.

I look after Casey and Hudson whenever Murray needs me to, and I do so with pleasure. Ivy and Murray separated in 2015, so the kids spend half of their time with one parent and the other half with the other. So much of everything I went through with Ivy and the company dispute led back to my rights to see her children. It was a truly horrific time but all of it was worth fighting for, just to be able to spend this time with her boys. My other granddaughter, Phoebe, has lived with me since 2022. I adore having her around. She helps me feel young and brings such a spark to my day. She's quite practical, loves cars and enjoys working on them.

With the boys, I've always tried my best to teach them about the world. Anything we're doing, whether that's watching television or messing around with the football, I'll encourage them to be curious, to ask questions. It's such an important way of thinking about the world, and I wish someone had been able to help me think this way when I was young. One afternoon we were watching some skit on TV about soccer players, with different dialogue dubbed over the top. The boys had chosen it and I was happy to go along. I love it when they teach me about the world – it works both ways. Anyway, the distorted voice-over on the screen suddenly announced, 'I've got crabs!' I snorted, and the boys looked up at me, completely oblivious. So, pausing the TV, I turned and explained exactly what they were talking about. Hudson screwed up his face in disgust. 'Ew, Nan, that's gross!' I thought it was very funny. Ruby thinks I tell them too much, but I think it's important.

You see, it gives a lot of power to a child to speak with them like an adult, to make their opinions feel worthy and interesting. I've always vowed to make sure they know that I think of them as individual people, whom I respect in their own right, separate from their parents. I want them to be able to come to me if they're ever in trouble, if they ever need help.

One evening we were having dinner together, just Casey, Hudson and I. I was telling them some story or other, I can't exactly remember the details, but I dropped in a side note about my lack of education, how I wasn't blessed in the intellect department. Hudson put down his fork and they both screeched. 'My god, Nan, you're the cleverest person we know!' Hudson said. I stopped speaking, my train of thought halted. He had no idea how much that meant to me, how many years of lacking self-confidence, struggles with basic tasks I'd put myself down about. But children are so innocent, so direct. If they think something, they say it, which is why it melted my heart so much. Brushing over his words, we carried on with our meal, chatting and laughing away. But I carry that inside me at all times now. When I'm doubting myself, I remember that, yes, maybe I wasn't academically gifted, but I am smart and I am clever. My grandchildren help me remember that.

I don't often think about my fears anymore. I've overcome so much adversity, had to face fear on a daily basis for so much of my adult life, that it has become something I try not to dwell on too much. Hudson, Casey and I were watching a video on YouTube, on Brightside, where the clip explores lots of questions for the viewers to engage with. It's usually a fun guessing game, something a bit more interactive than normal television. That afternoon it asked the question, 'What are you afraid of?' So I stopped the video and asked them both.

'I'm scared of the dark,' said one of them. 'I'm afraid of getting into trouble,' said the other. So I told them how I handle these problems when I'm scared, and how I find the best thing to do is to try and face your fears, to talk to someone you trust about them. It's wonderful how they open up so much, feel able to tell me these things. Another question that came up was what they do when they're upset. Of course, this one felt more important. Due to the nature of my family, the genetics that seem to wreak havoc throughout some of our lives, I've always had the nagging sense of worry that my grandchildren might be prone to mental health episodes. But so far, so good. They both replied that they listen to music, or play in their bedroom or in the garden with the football. I pressed on, asking, 'Do you ever try to hit something or hurt yourself?' 'No, of course not!' was the resounding answer, confusion flickering across their faces for a second.

I spoke to their father about the dark issue, just in passing. He met me with a look of surprise, and said he had no idea. It turned out that at Ivy's they slept with a nightlight but at their father's there was nothing. I don't know if they changed anything there, but I do know he was glad I'd told him. It's a privilege that they talk to me about these things. Of course, I have to be careful about what I say to their parents, I don't want them to feel as if I'm telling tales on them.

Sometimes they ask me about the war. Now I don't know where that's come from. I assume they just see my age and assume I was around then. It does make me chuckle though, they really have no comprehension of the larger scale of things before they were born.

I have a small scar on my arm that I got years ago when Hudson was little. He was about eighteen months old and we were all at a party at Sheryl's house. At this point she lived on a large property, with her son and grandchildren. There was space in the garden to camp out, so one summer's evening we all brought our tents. It was me and Robert, Ruby and her family, and Ivy, Murray and Hudson.

I was sitting in my tent, the door flaps fluttering in the light breeze, when I saw a blurry flash of little legs toddling along in front of me. We were pitched on a slight hill, with a drop-off leading to a fence at the end. As the sunlight filtered through the evening clouds, I watched as Hudson whirled his body, propelling himself full speed towards the drop. I sprung up out of the tent. He was hurtling closer and closer to the edge, his gleeful smile spread across his tiny features, completely unaware of the danger in front of him.

Leaping from where I stood, I dived towards him like I was going in for a football tackle, scooping him up and catching him in my arms. As I fell, I saw Murray running towards us, so I threw him over to my left as I hit the ground. Incredibly, Murray caught him. It was one of those moments that you can't believe happened like that, but I promise you it was true.

I rolled over, my arm bleeding and my head covered in mud. In fact, I had landed in the goat pen, on the little fence separating the garden from the paddock. Murray was laughing, his face crinkled up like a crisp packet. 'Why did you do that?' he spluttered between hysterical gasps. 'I just couldn't let him fall,' I replied, picking a stick out of my hair. I turned to see Sheryl's back disappearing into the house. She had apparently thought that was the end of me, that I'd be dead, so she'd run off. Classic Sheryl.

After that Ruby and Robert ran down towards me, picking me up and helping me inside. My face was a patchwork of scratches and scrapes and I looked like I'd been in a fight. Once she'd recovered from my near death, Sheryl sheepishly came out and cleaned me up. Every time I see that little scar it reminds me of that day and brings a smile to my face.

It was at this same house that I accidentally drugged Robert. Sheryl's granddaughter was turning twenty-one, so there was another little party. It was a fancy dress, so I remember being clad head to toe in some awful costume. Driving up, Robert started complaining that his head was sore. He was always getting headaches, so I'd taken to always having some painkillers on me.

I popped him a couple of Panadol and gave him a bottle of water. He took the medicine, throwing the pills back, and carried on driving.

Once we arrived at the party, I noticed he was looking rather tired, slumping down in his chair, his eyelids sagging and heavy. But he was always tired, so this wasn't particularly new. Anyway, we stayed for the party, had a wonderful evening and then got back into the car to drive home. I hadn't been drinking so I climbed in behind the wheel while Robert collapsed into the passenger seat. We arrived home and went to bed. I didn't think anything of it until a couple of days later, when I was rifling through my bag for another painkiller. But this time I pulled out two packets. Oh no. I realised that instead of Panadol I'd given Robert Restavit, a sleeping tablet. I laughed, covering my mouth with one hand. I didn't tell Robert for over a year. Needless to say, once he found out, he always checked the packet.

I went out on Melbourne Cup Day and, silly me, drank a lot of strong, adult, bubbly beverages that I wasn't used to. My friends saw me safely home around 3 pm and said goodbye as I wobbled into the house thinking a little lie down on my bed might be a good idea. By 6:30, I found myself completely naked sitting on the lounge wearing only a shower cap. I've no idea when I took my clothes off but when Phoebe came home, there I was. 'Oh, Nan,' she said.

Suddenly remembering that I had to put the sheets on her bed, I staggered through to her room still wearing nothing but a shower cap. Shooing me out of there, Phoebe told me to get in the shower. Once out of the shower, I had a gourmet meal of burnt toast – not that I would have cared – and went and

Me in my shower cap!

made Phoebe's bed while she had a shower. I was still naked and wearing only my shower cap when she reappeared, sighed and bundled me off to bed. I knew nothing of all this until Phoebe filled me in the next morning.

Phoebe: My nan

My god, the number of times I've bumped into Nan walking around the house naked. She really doesn't care what people think, she wants to be free to do as she pleases and is just so open and refreshing. It's one of the things I love the most about her. Seeing her follow her heart and live the way she wants inspires me to have that level of confidence and self-assurance that she has. The number of times I've gone to Nan for help, upset over something, and she's just sat there and listened have been plenty. She always knows what to say, helps me figure out the situation and how to feel better. She's built up my resilience so much over the years, taught me to be able to shrug off a problem and move on, not to worry so much about what everyone else thinks.

Even in my earliest memories Nan is there: my first bath, my school plays, birthday parties. She's been a constant in my life and I'm so grateful to have such a strong relationship with her. Moving in together last year has only made us closer and I feel so lucky to get to share this time with her. I don't know too much about her own upbringing, but I know she didn't have it easy back in England growing up or when my mother was young. But she has been the best grandparent I could have asked for, even when she was going through difficult times herself. Moving in with her has also strengthened my relationship with my mum and helped me understand her better.

I remember when everything went down with my aunty Ivy and the company. That was a hard time for everyone. I'd hear Nan and my mother on the phone for hours every day, could feel the tension seeping through her skin and hanging over every meal, every morning and evening. I worked for the company as well during my holidays but wasn't involved enough to really know everything that went on. But I could see how hurt Nan was and how deeply the betrayal cut her. But I could also see how strong she was. As the company dissolved, her relationship with Robert cracked and some of her friends weren't all there for her, but I saw how she became her own rock. I've never met a person who looked after themselves, supported themselves and managed to stay so strong. As you can see, I'm very proud.

She's always believed in me, even when she doesn't understand why I want things or do things. She's never really understood my love of cars, it's my life, but she knows it's my passion and that's enough for her to support me. Living together we support each other, help each other grow, at least that's how it feels. I know that I can count on Nan no matter what, and that is truly the best feeling in the world.

Chapter 15

Susan

That's me, my authentic self

I am finally content. I carried so much shame through my life – shame about my dyslexia, my body, my education – but now I have finally accepted myself for who I am. It feels damn good. I grew up with such a sense of distrust in everyone, men especially. It's followed me over the years, but as I've grown older it's gently begun to peel away. I think it was meeting Robert that really opened my heart up, allowed me to let other people in. It might not have been good for me at the time, but allowing myself to trust people feels so much healthier. Of course, I've been burnt, but now I throw myself into friendships, interactions and lean into my life, no longer cowering in the corner.

But there are still certain things that hang around, things I can't quite shake. I don't like sitting with my back to the door of a room. I use my spoon or a glass to look behind me in the reflection. I jump if someone makes a loud noise. It's these little things that persevere. I'm not scared anymore, but the physical manifestation of all those years of fear is still within me. I know it may seem like I've had a tough life, but it just feels normal. I've had so many wonderful experiences, visited incredible places and created a beautiful family. I'm grateful for the good things and I've moved on from the bad.

I'm part of a group called the Brisbane Bumblebees. There are around ten of us, all women, and we organise activities to go out and have fun. We buzz around the city, visiting new places, finding new things to do, I absolutely love it. I've come to appreciate friends a lot more in my recent years. Each of us has our own pet name. I originally suggested my own as 'Dumb Bee' but they weren't happy with that at all. So I settled on 'Bubbly Bee' instead. I've learnt to reframe my perception of myself, to look for my best traits rather than my worst. It's made my life a lot more enjoyable.

That's not to say I still don't do some rather laughable things. A couple of nights ago I was heading out to a trivia night, when I decided I'd take my bike. It's only around five kilometres but it was six o'clock and dark already. I hopped on my bike, pedalling through the streets, until after a few minutes my lights went out. My vision went black, my pupils dilating as they struggled to readjust my vision. After a couple of seconds everything came back into focus and I carried on pedalling, weaving through the dimly lit streets. After my evening, I cycled home again, like a bat in the dark night sky, invisible to the traffic around me. It was probably pretty dangerous. When I got home, I took a look at the lights to change the battery and, lo and behold, realised I'd flicked off the switch. I didn't even think to check. It's taken me years to accept that this is normal, though, that I'm not stupid and everyone makes mistakes.

I've mellowed a lot over the years, but I still have that burning fire inside me. There have been times when it was just ash, floating away in the wind, but it's now settled into soft embers. Every now and then a spark will ignite, and I'll be thrown into a wave of passion, but not as often as when I was younger. Recently I was at my women's network group, listening to a talk from Blue Care. The woman next to me kept playing on her phone, talking and making an unreasonable amount of noise. I couldn't hear a thing. Quietly I asked her to please stop, so the rest of us could listen. She didn't. A few minutes later I exhaled an exasperated 'Shush!' Still no change. Finally, I couldn't stand it anymore and before I knew it, I shouted, 'Oh for fuck's sake!' I even shocked myself. I hadn't meant to say it, the words had just erupted from my mouth, my mind fizzing with fury at this woman.

I apologised to the other ladies for swearing and tried to settle back down. I've always been loud, always had this energy, and sometimes I can't control it. But one woman that day thought it was brilliant. I'd noticed her walk in, took one look at her and just knew that I wanted to be her friend, that she looked fun. She said when she heard me snap, she realised it too. It's at moments like this that I'm proud to be myself, as the things I saw as my flaws for so long actually make me, me.

Friendship: A few words about Susan

Yvonne Fitzgerald, Honey Bee

I met Susan just over a year ago and I can safely say that her vibrant personality, sharp wit and positive nature make her an absolute joy to be with. Hearing her tales of her life shocked me. I didn't understand how someone who has been through so much could be so optimistic, but I realise now that it's the only way to keep going. We've experienced similar difficulties with our children and being able to talk to her about the challenges of mental health in the family has been a lifesaver. My brother has a disability, and completely out of the blue Susan volunteered to care for him while

I went on holiday for three weeks. Her kindness, resilience and inspiring drive are just some of the reasons I'm proud to call her my friend.

Nici Warby, Wanna Bee

I have found it quite difficult to sum up Susan, as she has so many sides, like the diamond she is. She is so resilient, a survivor through and through. She is generous, always helping out others, looking for ways to do her part. She can be like a bull in a china shop, loud and wild, throwing herself into her next project. She can also be gullible. But most of all she is loving. A patient, truly kind person who I feel privileged to call my friend. I'd sum her up as like a caramel chocolate eclair, hard on the outside but soft in the middle!

Glenda Wraight

I have known Susan for thirty-eight years. I met her through my mad sister-in-law (probably the only sane thing she ever did). Susan and I had an instant connection and have stayed friends ever since. We met when we were living in Housing Commission houses and would drop in for a cuppa and a chat very often. Our children and Ruby and John were around the same age. Whenever Sue and Ruby were popping over, John would make himself scarce. Of course, now they're married and have Phoebe.

Susan and I used to go on nights out together, sometimes to Hub Club or down the Valley streets, to look for our future husbands. Unfortunately, this wasn't quite meant to be, so we tried a dating agency instead. We realised we'd have to kiss a lot of frogs to find what we were looking for, so decided being our fabulous single selves was a far better option. We drifted apart for a few years after this but once we reconnected it was like absolutely nothing had changed. Sue is one of my most long-time friends and now part of my family.

Wendy Bond

Sue is a straightforward, no-nonsense, honest woman and everything she tells you has come straight from her heart. Her life and experiences are almost unbelievable and the positivity she carries around despite all she's been through is truly remarkable. When you read this book, imagine her London accent and know you'll be in for a wild ride.

Carol Sims, Zombie Bee

I met Susan a couple of years ago and she truly is one in a million. Her bubbly, friendly nature is infectious, and I always feel so uplifted in her company. She is an open-hearted, honest woman, who has experienced so much herself yet still finds the energy to help others. She helped me when I was struggling with my son's troubles, even when she was going through far worse; I don't know how she is able to give so much while coping with the obstacles in her own life. She never judges people and I feel immensely proud and honoured to call her my dear friend.

Elaine, Sweet Bee

Susan has travelled many paths throughout her life, paths many of us would never dare to tread. Despite all of the scars along the way, she has risen above them to shine. To those that pass her in the street she is a beautiful, happy, smiling, friendly woman, and it is only if you are a friend that you know her journey and what lies behind her smile.

Carolyn Veal, Queen Bee

I met Susan a couple of years ago before the Bumble Bees started. It was over a cuppa in a local coffee shop that I heard her extraordinary story for the first time. I was mesmerised. As I went to sleep that night, I couldn't shake off her tales of growing up in

London. Now, after knowing Susan for some time, I have found that she is quite an incredible woman. She is a woman who will try her hand at anything and has had such an interesting life. She has tried so many different jobs, overcome so many challenges and is one of the most fun, bubbly people I know.

Trudy Jardine

Susan is the most forgiving and non-judgemental person I know. I first met Susan when I came to view the house next door to her – a little over two years ago. At that time I was undecided as to what type of accommodation I wanted to move into after my home of ten years at Cannon Hill was sold. I had been looking at high-rise units in the Wynnum area but somehow knew that something was not quite right. Then a real estate agent brought me to the house next door to Susan. I didn't immediately fall in love with the street or the house, which was neat but not quite the design I had envisaged. Before long, Susan came over to say a friendly and incredibly welcoming 'hello' and almost immediately invited me into her house, which she clearly loves and is proud of. She took me through and explained the changes she and her husband Robert had made several years before, when they first moved in. She generously showed me the enormous potential of the house next door and said that it was such a lovely street to live in. Well, I signed an offer that day and two years later I have a lovely renovated house and a wonderful neighbour, Susan. I have to say she is both a wonderful neighbour and a dear friend. Over the months I have lived here Susan has shared her life story with me and it's amazing that she does not bear a bitter feeling towards any of the people who have hurt her deeply. She is such an inspiration.

Food has always been a source of both joy and despair for me. Growing up, we didn't have much at all. I have vague memories of roast dinners in Battersea: sizzling potatoes, roast meat and boiled greens. But in general, when I was young, food was about survival rather than pleasure. My brushes with starvation were commonplace and the panic of not knowing where the next meal would come from still pains me to this day.

My first real experience of cooking was when I moved out of the children's home and in with Max. I would make curries as they were simple and cheap, just throwing whatever we could afford into the pan, cooking it down to a soft stew. In Wellingborough, we had an apple tree in the garden, so I'd take the children outside to pick the fruit to make apple crumbles or pies. They were often acidic, sharp and tangy, but that was how the kids liked them.

It wasn't until I moved to Australia that I found real excitement in food. I moved on from curries to risottos, fancy salads and anything that seemed interesting. I even ate grasshoppers once. All the years I'd been forced to cook for Max suddenly evaporated into a bubble of steam and I began to use cooking to nourish rather than simply as a chore. My mother wouldn't cook for Jim when he was out at work, but he was a kind man and I liked him, so I often would. I think so much of showing your love can be done through food.

That being said, in the early days of Robert and my relationship, he once turned around and told me he liked his dinner around 5:30. I snorted, scoffing at his demand. I told him that if I was not hungry, I wouldn't be cooking and he would have to find another woman. I waited but he wouldn't leave. When I made him dinner, it was on my own terms, because I wanted to, not because he told me to. It took a while for him to understand why I was like that.

I also knew how food fuelled hatred. And drink, bad behaviour. Back in the UK whenever I went to visit Max's parents, Max's father would berate me, the same as his son. There was the expectation that a wife was little more than a servant, with the sole purpose of serving her husband. For years, I was crammed into this box, unable to break free. I could only fight back with tiny discrepancies, small acts of rebellion. One of these was poisoning Max's father. Every time he demanded a cup of tea, I would drip a single drop of bleach into his cup. Never enough to do any real damage, but that wasn't my intention. I just wanted to have some power back, to be able to inflict my own control over him.

Ruby and Jeffery are both excellent cooks. When they were teenagers and young adults, they helped with the cooking while I was at work. It really was a team effort and I love that they still cook to this day. I've tried to pass it down to my grandkids. We'll learn a recipe together, make it from scratch and eat it around the table. It's a real bonding effort and the looks of pure joy that smatter their faces warm my heart. Sometimes when they're coming around overnight, I'll call them up on the phone before, to ask what they want to eat. It's often butter chicken or tuna mornay; they really love those. I then ask them which one of them will cook it.

We used to have themed cooking nights. Ruby, Carol, Cindy and I, and our families, would all gather at one of our houses, choosing a nationality to cook food in the style of. Different countries would be scrawled onto tiny pieces of paper, and then we'd cluster round the table and draw them out of a hat. Once you'd picked your country, there was no swapping, you had to throw yourself into cooking a full meal for everyone from scratch. Those were wonderful dinners, everyone together, really putting in a lot of effort. I think very fondly of those evenings. We did this every month for a long time.

Wine is another thing I never really took an interest in until I came to Australia. Back in England we were too poor to drink. Of course, this didn't stop Max from going out with his friends, but for me it wasn't really an option. I would have liked one drink at Christmas or New Year but had no money for it. But when I came to Australia, I got a real taste for it. For the warm, safe feeling that accompanies it, the relaxation of a glass on rare occasions.

Surprisingly though, I've never sought solace in alcohol. So many people seem to get trapped trying to drown their worries in the liquid, but it just never occurred to me. Even at my worst it didn't cross my mind. A couple of beers or a glass of sweet wine is all I ever need. Just enough to get a bit silly, to have a laugh.

For someone who struggles so much with writing, it's unexpected how much I love to read. I feel at my safest when I have a book under my arm; I'll read anything. Max didn't let me read for so many years. He would snatch the book from between my fingers, flinging it across the room. He felt threatened by anything that gave me autonomy and independence.

At twenty-eight, when I finally started reading properly, I began with historical novels. I'm not sure why. I swiftly moved on to romance books and now I've settled into murder mysteries. It's strange, I'll a read a magazine on rare occasions, always starting on the last page, working my way towards the beginning. I'm not sure why I do this, but I always have done. Writing is still a challenge. My hand glides across the paper yet the words don't quite end up in the right place. But I've come to accept that now.

I'm not afraid of death, just of dying too early. I don't want my grandchildren to still be young, I want for them to be settled, to have lives of their own, that's my main fear. Given the choice, I'd rather have some notice, to give me a chance to say goodbye. I'd like to apologise properly to Ruby and this book will be my opportunity. Her childhood was very difficult, and she's done so much for me over the years; I wish I could have provided more for her.

I used to be afraid of being alone. Perhaps that's why I stuck with so many questionable people over the years, letting them stay in my life rather than pushing them away. But in the last few years, I've discovered the power of solitude. It's not that I don't want to be with other people, it's that I'm not dependent on anyone anymore. Seeing my family and friends brings such joy to my life, but I don't need them to validate me, to make me feel whole. I know that if I really needed to, I could disappear on my own and live out my life, content with my authentic self.

The fallout with Ivy and the company really defined who I could truly rely on. There were a few people whom I counted as some of my closest allies, but they weren't there for me when I needed them. That hurt for a while. Now, I know the people I trust really do have my back, they're people I can call if Jeff's in a bad way and I need to vent. People who check in on me to see how my mental health is holding up. These people demand to be my emergency contact when I'm filling in a form. Ruby and John both really stepped up for me, and for that I will be forever grateful. Family is complicated but friendship is too, and they are the two most important things in the world.

I am scared of heights though. I never used to be. Skipping across the train tracks in Battersea station and leaping from rooftops over dingy alleyways formed so much of my childhood. I remember the exhilarating feeling of danger, the fleeting sense of flying as I sailed through the air, always landing in a scruffy tussle in the dust. The fear of heights began on my honeymoon with Robert. We were on a cruise, drifting across the ocean on this giant vessel. Being the joker he was, he called out to me, 'Don't go near the edge, I might just push you over!' Of course, he was joking, but I wasn't going to risk it. You hear about these accidents on boats all the time. I kept my distance from the thin railings, peering down the vertical drop into the churning swathes of blue, pulling and writhing below. A shudder rippled up my spine. I wasn't going anywhere near that.

Another time we were skiing in Japan. As the chairlift spun round, scooping us into its arms and chugged on up the mountain I realised we were going the wrong way. My legs dangled, small and skinny against the white expanse of rock looming below. We had taken the lift right to the top, right to the steepest, thinnest runs. I swallowed, fear rising in my throat. Glancing over at Robert I could see he looked rather pale, beads of sweat forming on his lip. Cautiously we set off. After all, there was only really one option. The sharp twists and icy turns loomed in front of us, steep ravines turning out to be the designated paths. I watched someone glide past, seemingly graceful and controlled, until they zipped straight off the run, colliding with the tall trees in a powdery mess. I gritted my teeth, tensing my whole body as we skidded down the mountain.

It took me hours to get down. When I finally arrived at the bottom, my legs were weak, my body shaking. I was so dehydrated, I downed a can of some sickly, sweet drink, which clung to my mouth in a cloying film. I hate soft drinks, but I just couldn't get enough of it. I was quite shaken up. I didn't touch the mountains for a couple of days, as I needed some time to recover. But I knew I'd still go back, would still try again. The best thing about being scared about something is learning to overcome it. That's what I've worked so hard at my whole life.

I've definitely become more adventurous over the years. I've been parasailing, ridden on an underwater motorbike, climbed up a volcano. The volcano really was something else. It started on another cruise. We were meant to go to Fiji but there was a hurricane, so we diverted to Vanuatu. By this point I'd been there a couple of times before so wasn't interested. I was with Robert and my two sisters-in-law and I was ready for an adventure.

We stepped off the ship as it docked and Robert and I hopped straight into a taxi to the airport. As we boarded this tiny flight to Tanna island I glanced at the rickety wheels, the battered casing of the plane. This is a real adventure, I thought, as the attendant took my hand luggage to weigh it, making sure this tiny handbag didn't disrupt the plane's weight capacity. Then we were weighed, something that made me lose a bit of confidence. He asked if we had anywhere to stay and we told him we didn't. Kindly, he called up a few places, booking us a night at The Chicken Coop. The plane was old and the runway even older; in fact, on Tanna there wasn't even a proper landing strip, just empty scrub.

As we arrived all I could see was black. Ash filtered through the air, coating the moonscape surface of the rock. There was no colour, just a white sea of dust. It was beautiful. After we dropped our bags at the accommodation, we jumped into a truck that went winding up the side of the volcano. I could feel the shudders underneath me, the ground itself breathing and coughing. As we stepped off the vehicle, the driver turned around to us and shouted, 'Watch out for rocks, someone was killed by a falling piece last week.' And with that he drove away. We stood staring at the mountain, gleeful wonder radiating from my soul. I felt so alive, so free being this close to something so powerful. The wind snatched at my body, whipping my hair and grabbing at my clothes. The hot ashy smell filled my nostrils and as we reached the top and I looked out into the pit, I saw the lava dancing below. It spluttered and bubbled, erupting small clouds of fire.

After scrambling down the mountain, we collapsed. Ash had settled into every tiny crevice of my body, but there was no hot water. Our accommodation was a windowless dormitory, with no fridge, no warm water and nothing much else. Robert jumped into the shower, his yelps in the icy water piercing the ringing in my ears. But I couldn't follow him – cold water is the one other thing I'm afraid of. So I just went to bed, my teeth still crunching with ash.

The next day, we woke up starving so we went to look for something to eat. We wandered across the beach, hoping to find a small shop. As we walked, I began to notice we were being followed. Men lined the sandy shores, some holding machetes, and one by one they began to trail behind us. Fear trickled through me as I realised what was happening. My blood froze. I clung to Robert, who stood up straight, his broad shoulders and strong back puffing up, trying to look harder than he was. Eventually we reached the shop, now with a collection of men following us, not doing anything, just watching.

Robert pushed open the door, offering them to go in first. 'No, no,' they replied. We picked a couple of things to eat and still these men followed. It was then that I raised the courage to look into their eyes. Expecting to see hatred, anger, some sort of threat, I instead was met with curiosity. In fact, none of them were even looking at me. They were staring intently at Robert, their eyes sorting through the maze of tattoos that covered his arms and legs. This was what they were actually interested in, not us. A wave of relief rolled through me, as I gently signalled to Robert to leave, realising that everything was okay. He met my gaze, saw me relax and followed me out.

Once we'd eaten, we picked up our bags and went back to the tiny airport. The building was smaller than a garage and dogs skidded across the potholed runway, Bundling onto the plane we sat in our seats, watching out the window as the tiny island shrank into the vastness of the sea. Robert turned to me, his teeth chattering. 'Are you cold?' he asked. I was not. It was sweltering. The noise was deafening, the thrums of the engine fighting over the searing propellers.

When the plane landed and we stood up to exit, I turned around to check I had not left anything on my seat. In that final glance Robert saw a fair-sized hole right where we'd been sitting. I gasped with laughter, my hand flying up to my mouth.

We went straight to a restaurant and then boarded the cruise ship again. It felt like we'd been away for days, not a mere twenty-four hours. It's adventures like this that I love to look back on, to remind myself of all the extraordinary things I've done. I still have a piece of rock that I picked up at the volcano. These are the things I know I'll look back on, on my deathbed. The good bits, not the bad.

A letter from James Culshaw, given to Susan on a trip to Finland in 2023.

There is a very rare type of person who can be dragged through the sewer of life and still smell of roses. Who can walk through fire, the hell of life and not be burnt or disfigured, and who can be frozen by society but remain warm of heart. They seem to have an endless capacity to be kind to others and incapable of bitterness or self-pity by blaming others. It is as if they have a higher moral code in their DNA to dismiss the trivial and focus on the essential.

Susan Norman is the epitome of this person, a privilege to meet and an inspiration – a barometer to put one's own life in perspective.

www.ingramcontent.com/pod-product-compliance
Lightning Source LLC
Chambersburg PA
CBHW052358030726

47599CB00014B/1122